DEPTH ASTROLOGY

An Astrological Handbook

Volume 1

Introduction

By

Gargatholil

Corrected and Revised

ISBN: 9781791599577

Table of Contents

ACKNOWLEDGMENTS

I briefly wish to acknowledge the influences and contributions of several writers whom I have never met but who have shaped my thinking and informed my knowledge of depth astrology. These include Alan Leo for a general introduction to astrology in his *Esoteric Astrology*; the great Dane Rudhyar, particularly for his work in the interpretation of the astrological houses; Liz Greene, especially for her work with Saturn; Frances Sakoian and Louis Aeker for their work on the quincunx; Stephen Arroyo; Donna Cunningham and more whom I have forgotten.

PREFACE

The natural horoscope is a mandala. The natural horoscope is also the complete astrological symbology of signs, houses, planets, points and aspects. As mandala, the center of the natural horoscope is, as all centers are, the One. From the One manifest the Twelve (the Zodiacal signs and houses). Each has its own center, which is its Essence.

The Essences of the Twelve are each a different (differentiated) reflection of the One—Its emanations. So, too, are the ten planets and the five points. Each of these Essences is differentiated from the One and from each other by their Attributes—Elements, Modalities (the three *gunas* of Hindu thought) and Qualities. These Attributes are then manifested on various planes, or levels of differentiation. It is this differentiation, on various levels, that result in the variety of qualities and functioning represented by the astrological symbols.

The more undifferentiated the manifestation of the astrological symbol, the purer is the expression of its Essence. Also, the more undifferentiated it is, the more the description of its Essence is ineffable. As the Attributes become more differentiated, they become more concrete and material. Also, the qualities symbolized by an astrological symbol are more strongly associated with the ego as the astrological symbol is actualized on planes of greater differentiation (lower levels of consciousness).

As the astrological symbols are manifested at levels of greater diversity and greater material content, the consciousness or spirituality associated with their attributes and qualities lessens. Multiplication of meaning is a movement away from Wholeness, away from Spiritual Oneness. At an outer ring of the astrological mandala, the qualities and attributes symbolized by the planets, signs, houses and aspects begin to contain tangible quantities of Emptiness. This Emptiness is the self-destructive polarity of the astrological mandala. It is born of attachment to the ego, which is illusion (i.e., the ego itself is an Emptiness).

2

Thus, the mandala becomes darker and darker as it moves away from the Light (which is the Center). The growing darkness is self-destruction or annihilation. In the end, all the astrological symbols manifest at the negative polar extreme in a self-destructive mode. Thus, ironically, there is a unity of meaning at both polarities of the astrological spectrum—undifferentiated Oneness at the positive pole (or Center) and self-destruction at the negative pole.

In the chapters that follow, the astrological symbols found in the horoscope are analyzed consistent with the framework presented above. Before describing just how the analysis proceeds, I want to discuss the idea of the "astrological symbol." Not long ago, with Dane Rudhyar and others, a more mature astrology developed in the Western world— an astrological school that I would label "depth astrology." In this school, the old and erroneous ideas—that physical planets caused or influenced events in peoples' lives through their motions and positioning in relation to the Zodiac, that the arrangement of planets in the natal horoscope determined who you were and what would happen to you, that the primary value of astrology was to predict the future—in short, all of the practices by which astrology had been duly labeled an unscientific superstition—were abandoned to a great extent.

These outmoded ideas were replaced by an awareness that the physical relationships of the planets and Zodiacal signs in relation to the Earth were symbolic of psychological and archetypal forces acting within and through the personal psyche. These pioneers of depth astrology realized that the correspondences between the observed movements and placements of the planets, on the one hand, and the inner or outer circumstances that were being experienced, on the other hand, are synchronistic, and not causal, in nature.

Much of the writing about the meaning of the astrological symbology (in terms of personality, psychological and emotional forces, and self-development) has been influenced, directly or indirectly, by Jungian psychology. The analysis of the astrological symbols presented in this work is consistent with this approach.

There have also been, chiefly in reaction to the labeling of astrology as unscientific, some attempts to ground astrology in an objective, observation-based, scientific framework. While I have no quarrel with this approach, my own approach has been to deal with the astrological symbols *as* symbols. A symbol, as I have defined it, is a content-holder for an idea or a group of related ideas. As such, symbols can be manipulated and juxtaposed to derive meanings that are specific to the particular combination of symbols being considered.

The process of exploring the astrological symbol set is admittedly intellectual, intuitive and subjective. It is more art than science. Its validity rests on the Platonic idea that this consensual reality (i.e., the material world) is a copy of the Form of a Reality that exists in the world of Idea. As above, so below. If the astrological horoscope is a symbol-map deriving from a higher Reality, then an intuitive perception of the meaning of that "map" should be possible. This leads to an intellectual construct that, hopefully, represents a valid functionality.

Please note that I have claimed "a valid functionality" and not "the valid functionality." One key idea that underpins the analysis of the astrological symbology presented in this work is that, while an Absolute may exist, *this* reality is relativistic. There is no correct point of view, only valid points of view. Thus, while the analysis presented here is not objective, I do believe that it is pragmatic. If a valid construct "works," then it is valuable to the individual(s) for whom it is useful.

It is my hope that the analysis presented in this book works to enhance self-understanding and self-direction for those individuals attuned to it. You will hopefully enhance your understanding of others, as well. Particularly, I hope that this work is useful to a group of practicing astrologers.

INTRODUCTION

The basic format used in this work is to juxtapose the astrological symbols from two symbol sets and explore the meaning derived from this juxtaposition. The sets used are the planets and major points (from here on, simply "planets"), the signs and the houses. A juxtaposition of more than two becomes too cumbersome, both in terms of simplicity and the number of permutations. Of course, in actual chart interpretation, the astrologer must consider multiple juxtapositions and deal with these intuitively. The book explores meanings for two juxtaposed sets in hopes of aiding the interpretation of the multiple juxtapositions that are actually found in the horoscope.

The juxtapositions of the symbol sets that are explored in this work are:

- planets in signs

- planets in houses and

- planets in aspect to each other.

Before discussing the juxtapositions of these astrological symbol sets, we need to explore the meanings of the each of the astrological symbols themselves. Definitions of the essence of each symbol are given later in this Introduction. Prior to this, there is a discussion of the essential meanings of the components of the astrological symbols—the elements, modalities and geometric relationships.

The analyses of the juxtaposed astrological symbols presented on this website generally follow a defined format. Each analysis opens with a brief, keyword definition of the essential meaning or dynamic of the symbol set. The paragraphs that follow then elaborate on this essential meaning, generally bringing out the dynamics inherent in the juxtaposition of the two symbols.

Because the essences of the symbols themselves are complex and ineffable, I do not attempt to capture the entire meaning of the symbol set in this capsulated form. The initial definition of meaning of a symbol set may be more or less pregnant, depending upon the particular symbols being juxtaposed and, often, the strength or poignancy of their interaction. Nevertheless, this serves as a "jumping off point" for further discussion.

Planets in signs, planets in houses and planets in aspects are handled somewhat differently as these discussions progress. Planets in signs are sometimes given a treatment that is simpler than that given to planets in houses and planets in aspects. The Zodiacal signs are primarily symbolic of qualities. As they move through the signs, the planetary symbols take on "color" from those signs. It is as if the same essence is seen through different colored lenses as the planets pass through the Zodiac. Though there may be some dynamic interaction between planets and signs, the major phenomenon that occurs at the symbolic level is that the planetary function takes on qualities associated with the Zodiacal sign. It is analogous to a person putting on a robe. The dynamic interactions (for instance, between essence of the planetary symbol or the functions that it symbolizes and the element and/or modality of the Zodiacal sign) suggest whether this robe fits well or whether the wardrobe clashes.

Throughout the analysis of planets in signs, the essential function symbolized by the planet is portrayed as manifesting through the coloration of the Zodiacal sign to produce qualities or personality characteristics. This may be viewed as analogous to white light being shot through a prism. Except, in this case there are fifteen varieties of white light and twelve types of prisms. Each of the 180 manifestations is unique.

Each analysis of planets in signs gives a taste of the representative qualities that emanate from the interaction of the planetary essence and the Zodiacal coloration. The resonance and timbre of function and coloration express themselves in the personality. What is expressed or symbolized by a particular planet in a particular sign is, first of all, a certain facet (or function) of the psyche and then the way in which this facet operates or exists within the psyche or personality is overlaid onto this function.

What then, is to account for the diversity of personality and character that is found among people with the same planetary placement in a sign? Bear in mind, again, that we are not assuming that causality operates between the astrological chart and the individual's personality. Rather, what we observe is a synchronicity between the expression and manifestation of the personality and the layout of the astrological chart. The chart is symbolic or representative, not deterministic, of the personality and psyche. The reader is left to his/her own beliefs concerning what the essential determinates of the personality and psyche are, in reality.

So, we will answer this question from a symbolic and structuralist perspective. To a certain extent, of course, one may say that the differences among individuals are inherent in the individual astrological chart, because there is the influence of all the other astrological combinations and these differ among individuals, except for those born at the same moment in the same location of the Earth. Thus, there are the subtle differences of degree placement, declination, progression, asteroids, etc. However, although all this produces much more diversity and very specific astrological "directions," there are still many instances in which many people have practically the same astrological chart and their personalities and psyches are very different from one another. One may argue the role of nurture, of course.

In my own view, the role played by the major astrological symbols in explaining the shape and dynamics of the individual personality is paramount and overwhelms the subtler shadings found in the chart. Also, in my own view, nurture is as much a captive of whatever deterministic force is symbolized in the astrological chart and is shaping the personality and psyche as is nature. I would propose that the individual differences that are manifested when different people share a common astrological horoscope are primarily the result of differences in "attunement."

"Attunement" may be defined as an inner affinity for certain expressions, certain facets and certain levels of consciousness/positivity/negativity that may be manifested from the central Idea represented by the astrological symbol set. This, "I believe, is a deterministic affinity, in that it is innate within the individual. This does not preclude this attunement being acted upon, modified, enhanced or suppressed by external events or environment. Nor does it preclude the modifying how this attunement is manifested through the internal action of the individual (i.e., self-development). Everyone has a unique attunement and, symbolically, it is the individual's attunement to the range of possibilities symbolized in his/her astrological chart that make him/her a unique individual.

Planets symbolize psychological functions within the human consciousness. In the essential keyword meaning of the symbol set, the essential planetary function is qualified by an essential Zodiacal quality. Again, the actual essences of these symbols are ineffable and in choosing to put one central meaning into words, I am necessarily excluding others from the verbal description. My aim is that other meanings associated with the essential meaning of the symbol set—and just as valid—will emanate from this central point in the succeeding discussion.

The discussion of the essential keyword meaning of the symbol set begins with a brief elaboration of the meaning of the symbol set. This may include a discussion of certain psychological needs suggested by the symbol set. It may also include an examination of the harmony and/or dissonances suggested by the interaction of the planetary symbol and the various components of the Zodiacal sign—element, modality, glyph, etc.

This is followed by a set of positive and opposing negative qualities associated with the placement of the planet in that sign. For planets symbolizing multiple functions (having multiple aspects of the essential function), the qualities are categorized by function. These qualities are generally given in key-word fashion, although for some planets, longer explanations of their qualities in particular signs are called for.

The "traditional" (and outmoded) concept that characterizes certain planets) as "good" or "bad", "positive" or "negative" is rejected in this analysis. Rather, the use of positive and negative poles to describe the qualities associated with the planets in the various Zodiacal signs implies that every planet and its placement in each Zodiacal sign symbolically manifests along an ethical continuum in which positive and negative expressions of the essence of the astrological symbol are equally possible. If the reader wishes, he/she can replace the concept of an "ethical continuum" with that of a "practical continuum," since negative character and personality qualities generally produce dysfunctional results. Thus, the characteristics of positivity and negativity are functions of a person's attunement and not inherent in the planetary symbols themselves. Thus, Saturn can be your "friend" and

Venus your "enemy," all depending upon your level of consciousness and attunement.

Following this, there is an exploration of the essential meaning of the symbol set at the level of its "Transcendent Potential." The Transcendent Potential is manifested at a level of consciousness that tends in its direction toward selflessness (i.e., the center of the astrological mandala). More specifically, it is representative of the transcendence of the lower self through conscious action. Because such a transcendence is a convergence of the self toward the One, the various planet-sign combinations necessarily produce many similarities in symbolic meaning at this level, although these meanings are still colored by Zodiacal sign and are representative of the planetary function.

Next, there is an exploration of the essential meaning of the symbol set at the level of its "Insecurity." There is a basic premise that insecurity is produced through the attachment of the ego to the realm of illusion. At some subconscious level, each person knows that the consensual reality of the relative plane is unreal and that that to which he/she is attached is impermanent and must ultimately disappear. This knowledge produces fear, insecurity about the reality of self and its personality and an urge to hold on to the ego's attachments and defend the ego against its inevitable meaninglessness. This results in negative behavioral and personality traits.

Transcendent Potential and Insecurity represent the extreme manifestations of the astrological symbol set.

Finally, there is a discussion of how the qualities associated with the planet through each Zodiacal sign may be modified when astrological aspects to other planets are taken into consideration. Aspects can often affect the dynamics and meaning indicated by a planet's placement in a sign. This analysis makes the assumption that there will usually be a dominant planet in an astrological aspect that will have more "influence" on its partner than the degree to which it, itself, is "influenced." Therefore, both the aspecting influence of the planet in a particular sign on other planets and the affect of being aspected by an outer planet are discussed.

You are correct if you have deduced that the analysis of the astrological system presented here assumes a certain worldview and philosophy of Existence. It is my duty at this point to the reader to make these assumptions explicit, at least in brief. I recognize that there is an almost unbridgeable divide between those who participate, in some form, in the worldview that is assumed in this analysis of astrological symbols and those who reject it. Included in the latter category are those for whom this worldview is so foreign that they cannot even formulate it enough to consciously reject it. I do not mean here to imply any spiritual "superiority" on the part of those who share the worldview presented here, merely a difference in worldview.

First of all, the worldview underlying this work assumes that there is a Divine Force or Divine Essence and that this Divine is the ultimate goal of human existence. In the Reality of Eternity, there is no separation between the human soul and the Divine, nor can there be because only the Divine really exists. Thus, the Goal of human life— and the ultimate goal toward which all of the astrological symbols point--can be further specified: to reunite the human consciousness with the Divine Consciousness.

The pole opposite this extreme positive is the ego, which stands in the way of reaching this Goal. While the positive and necessary function of the ego, from the psychological perspective, is recognized, it is attachment to the ego and to the attachments of the ego that impede progress toward the Goal and are the ultimate source of all negativity and negative experience in the world.

In between the two extremes of selfless transcendence and obsessive egotism, there exists the domain of relativity--the consensual reality. Here human souls are born and play out their "existence." It is a realm of extreme multiplicity and diversity. It is a realm of conflict and harmony. It is a realm of action, of feelings and of thoughts. "Life" as we know it occurs in this realm. Its denizens are more or less conscious of the Divine and more or less enslaved by their egos.

Nothing in this realm has any absolute reality. The body is a mere covering. The personality is a more subtle covering. The personality has been conditioned from birth and continues to be conditioned by a variety of external forces. That which is conditioned are the various psychological functions that are symbolized by the planets. This conditioning must be overcome before the Goal can be achieved, or as a simultaneous part of achieving the Goal. The overcoming of a person's conditioning and his/her liberation from the ego is called self-realization or self-actualization.

A person is not free until all mental and emotional conditioning is transcended and he/she perceives the Divine Reality with his/her unaided inner eye. Free will is an illusion, at least while one is subject to his/her conditioning. Traditional astrology rests upon a premise that external events and circumstances are also predetermined, or predestined. However, the use of astrology to predict these events and circumstances and "know your future" is ultimately of no value to one who is pursuing the goal of self-realization and God-realization. That person's task in life is to go through his/her *karma*.

The concepts of karma and reincarnation are used, but are not necessary, in the analyses of the South Node, North Node and, to a certain extent, Saturn. For those readers who do not accept reincarnation and/or predestination, I believe that the explanations can still make sense. Free will is certainly a "reality" on the relative plane of existence. We all experience choice and our choice appears, more or less, to be free. Sufficient conditioning takes place during the present life to "explain" the presence of innate tendencies, talents and habits so that it is not necessary to look to past lives for the source of such conditionings.

You are sure to detect a basic moral assumption that runs through the analysis. This is that it is humanity's duty and highest aim to seek union with the One, to return to his/her Divine Source, to know him/herself, which means to know his/her Higher Self and to become fully conscious of the Divine. This very statement, of course, assumes that human beings are microcosms of the Divine macrocosm and that there is, in fact, no difference in essence between the human soul and the Divine, only a difference in consciousness. This, in turn, presumes a recognition that human beings are not the body, nor even the personality.

The personality can be seen as a covering, an accouterment. It is a thing apart from the soul, although one is indelibly attached, as it were, to one's personality during this lifetime. The structure and fabric of this covering of personality finds its symbolic representation in the astrological symbol set. However, as a person ascends in consciousness and approaches the Divine, his/her attachment to the personality becomes less and less. As he/she becomes less bound by this attachment, he/she partakes more and more in the universality of human qualities.

The corollary to the moral ideal presented above is that anything which takes us away from this goal is "less desirable" in the moral scale. This is a bitter pill, for we are all attached to "other Gods"--to numerous things, personalities, situations, beliefs, etc. that distract us from our moral purpose in life.

In fact, most people will at least make some progress toward this purpose. To the extent that you have a spiritual dimension, you are making progress toward this goal and this, rather than the goal's achievement, is what is important. Perhaps, it is not quite fair to expect the total transcendence of ordinary life. One may justly say that such a total transcendence is the mark of that rare individual, the complete mystic, and that this cannot be morally expected of everyone.

It is one thing to fail to progress toward the supreme purpose of life or to make little progress toward this goal. It is quite another to head in the opposite direction. The analysis presented in this work assumes that any behavior and attitude that is grounded firmly in ego--in an unwillingness to consider others' needs and the consequences of one's actions on others--is a sign of a fundamental insecurity. This supposition presupposes that, deep within the subconscious, each individual knows the Truth. It is this subconscious knowledge of Truth and the individual's unwillingness or inability to acknowledge that Truth that propels him/her into negative thoughts and behavior. Such negative and even perversely self-destructive behavior is generally a defense mechanism to protect the ego from confronting the Truth and being forced to abandon the illusory life that the person is leading.

Thus, self-indulgence, running after the sensory pleasures of the world at the sacrifice of human and social values and blatantly egoistic behavior are all signs of an obstinate moral rebellion. Lest this statement appear too judgmental, let me say that in most cases—and in all cases from some perspectives—the person who engages in such behavior has no choice. He/she is responding to the conditioning that has trapped him/her in an illusion.

This, then, is the philosophical and moral basis for the analysis of the astrological symbol set that is presented in this work. These assumptions also have guided how the analyses have been structured and presented. The basic description of the qualities and likely behaviors that are symbolized by each planet-in-sign combination represents the middle ground of ordinary existence in which the personality has some "reality." The Transcendent Potential points in the direction of the supreme human purpose. Insecurity describes someone who is fleeing from his/her Transcendent Potential and is trapped in the web of illusion.

Can astrology offer any real assistance to the individual, in no matter what state of consciousness he/she is living? The problems arising from predestination aside, it is hoped that this may be the case. Looking at the astrological symbolism may help in the diagnosis of the cause or dynamics of a negative psychological complex or behavior pattern. A corrective direction can also be indicated, provided the individual has the will to overcome his/her problem(s). Recognizing the transcendent potential inherent in an astrological symbol holds the potential to galvanize even one who is entrapped in his/her own insecurities, providing a ray of light to show the Way. For the individual existing in an ordinary state of consciousness, a study of the astrological symbol set may provide him/her with a greater understanding of his/her self and his/her world. A clearer understanding of the personality may be a step in gaining greater understanding of the Reality of Self. Greater understanding is also likely to result in greater peace of mind and an ability to make better decisions in life.

Basic Astrological Symbols

We now turn to an exploration of the meaning of the basic astrological symbols as they relate to the symbol set of planets in signs. This will begin with the planets. This will be followed by brief discussions of the elements, modalities and houses, followed by a more in-depth discussion of the signs. I use this order because it parallels how I perceive the astrological symbology to be constructed, or derived. In particular, it is my view that the signs are largely a composite of the other astrological symbols and that, therefore, it is necessary to talk about all of them, to some degree, in order to understand the meaning of the signs.

The planets (in which category we will include the calculated points) symbolize various psychological functions. These functions then relate to the meaning of the houses and the signs. The elements and modalities also relate to the meanings of the houses and signs. Finally, the houses, which symbolize areas of life experience, resonate to the meaning of the signs. The signs, then, take their meaning from a composite of other astrological symbols, adding to this their own mythological/glyphic symbol-meanings.

The Planets

The Sun

The Sun symbolizes the function of essential Being or consciousness. This awareness of self is central to the psyche and the personality. This centrality is symbolized by the Sun's glyph—a circle with a dot at the center. Thus, the Sun is recognized as one of the three major planets/points of the astrological system.

Although the Sun symbolizes the essence of Being within the individual, this essence is not clearly or directly grasped by most people. What most people perceive, generally, is their essence refracted onto the level of personality and ego-self. The Sun, then, comes to symbolize not the inner Self, but the outer self. In completing the statement "I am," most people do not say "That I am," but rather list a composite of qualities and attachments. This composite, we call "me." It is this me-ness that the Sun comes to symbolize in most people.

The qualities attached to me-ness are the qualities by which we defines ourselves. This is why the Sun sign has become such a ubiquitous indicator of astrological personality for most people. In the concept of self that is symbolized by the Sun, we find our identity. If we implicitly believe that the consensual reality is *the* reality, we will conceive this identity to be autonomous and unified. Being autonomous and unified, it is preeminent. The dot at the center of the circle is what is emphasized and this dot is viewed, effectively, as "the center of the universe" (the outer circle in the Sun's glyph).

To be relative and diversified means to lose the supremacy of the self, for the self now becomes contingent on a variety of factors. This relativity is our real condition—as symbolized by the multiplicity of planets found in different signs in different houses in different aspects to each other. This is also symbolized in the Sun's glyph by the central

15

dot's relationship to the infinity of points making up the circumference of the circle. We are blind to our real condition, however. We do not realize that the dot is central only because of its relations to the circumference. "I am me," we say and "me" is who functions in the material world and takes on all of those qualities that are identified with the self.

Although there is confusion, at this level, between the self (represented by the Sun) and the personality, it is the element of self-consciousness that is dominant and not the element of "qualities" when the function symbolized by the Sun is being analyzed. No matter how associated with his/her qualities a being may be, his/her being is still the central focal point--the point of consciousness through which he/she exists in the world. The qualities attached to this point of consciousness are those qualities which we identify with ourselves. They remain qualities that we possess—we are not those qualities.

The Sun symbolizes "is-ness." This is-ness is the actor, but action is not its primary function. It is the observer, but observation is not its primary function. It is the thinker and feeler, but thinking and feeling are not its primary function. Its primary function is to be and this beingness is clothed in the robe of "who I am."

The more our being is manifested in the world, the more this beingness, symbolized by the Sun, is "subject" to the influences or qualities symbolized by the astrological sign, house and aspects attached to it. As a person transcends his/her personal self, the Sun comes to symbolize more and more a state of pure consciousness. Just as the physical Sun is a vehicle through which light shines into the [otherwise] darkness of the solar system, so the astrological Sun symbolizes that point of consciousness, which is the self, through which Light shines into the darkness of the material universe. To reach back out of attachment to that darkness and become whole again in that Light—which is the Being of everyone—is the transcendent goal of humanity. In doing so, the individual becomes Self-realized. In other words, we realize fully that our body, mind, emotions and personality are not our real self. We then become united with and aware of our Real Self.

The Sun—which in the physical world is a hot, fiery globe—is most associated with the fire element. It rules the fire sign, Leo, and is at home in the other fire signs, as well. The fire element that is associated with the Sun tends to give its beingness a more active, rather than a contemplative, quality.

16

The Moon

The Moon has a host of meanings, each deriving from its essential representation of the subconscious aspect of the human psyche. Sun and Moon have long been archetypical symbols of Duality. The Sun traditionally is seen as the "positive", "active", "masculine" force while the Moon traditionally represents the "negative", "passive", "feminine" force. If the Sun symbolizes the individual's consciousness and Being, the Moon symbolizes the individual's subconscious (or unconscious) and Not-Being.

Paradoxically (dualities have a habit of creating paradoxes), if one is still at that stage of consciousness where he/she considers his/her personal self (Sun) to be real, the Moon represents a significantly wider and more inclusive "psyche-scape" than does the Sun, for the Moon symbolically opens out into the vast subconscious world which seems unlimited in comparison with sense-bound consciousness of the "me." When, however, we come into the full and transcendent realization of our Being, the area of the psyche symbolized by the Moon can now be viewed as limited. This may be symbolized by the fact that, in the night sky, the Moon is the brightest object, yet when the Sun shines, it fades and disappears.

All of what the Moon symbolizes astrologically can be viewed in the context of this interplay between the Universal Unconscious and the personal subconscious. When the Moon is seen as Universal Unconscious, the world of consciousness springs from this psychic medium. We have called the sense-based, linearly logical world that is consciously perceived by the mass of humanity, and is equated with the physical world, the world of "consensual reality." Consensual reality is born out of, grounded and rooted in the Universal Unconsciousness. Thus arises the Moon's association with rootedness and foundations.

The Moon represents the cultural context within which the individual is rooted. It is symbolic of one's heritage and of all things in the past, for the past, collectively, brings about and conditions all things in the present. The heritage and traditions that surround us, the society that we are born into and the collective weight of all of our experiences and associations condition our consciousness. Rather than experiencing direct perception and pure consciousness, we experience conditioned consciousness. It is consciousness (Light), with all of its potential,

17

but—like the Moon's light—it is reflected off of and affected by all of the objects with which the mind has association. Just as the night sky is lighted by the reflected light of the Moon, so the night of the material world is lighted only by the pale reflected light of conditioned consciousness.

The conditioning of consciousness is not merely abstract. This conditioning permeates our personality and self-in-this-world. How we react to various situations and stimuli, our natural mode of behavior and our habits and routines are all associated, astrologically, with the Moon. All of the ways in which we act without conscious consideration, automatically, can be viewed astrologically as being symbolized by the Moon and its placements in the chart. The Moon also symbolizes instincts and drives, which derive from the personal subconscious' conditionings and motivations.

Another metaphor that can be derived from the image of the world of consensual reality manifesting out of the Universal Unconscious is that of birth. As the Sun is associated with Being, the Moon is associated with Becoming. Thus, there is Moon-image involved in all types of organic processes in which things come into being, grow and die. The phases of the physical Moon are symbolic of the natural and cyclic order of things—the constant round of birth and death that permeates the consensual reality. If the mythological symbol for the Sun's essence is the Fire God, the Moon is represented by the Earth Mother Goddess.

Thus, we derive the Moon's astrological symbolism for motherhood and, through motherhood, for family. The mother-image brings together several strands symbolized by the Moon. The mother is, traditionally and still in most families, the primary transmitter of heritage—the link between the individual and his/her collective past. Mothers also have a tremendous power to condition their children, as the phrase "my mother's voice inside my head" implies. Motherhood is also very much associated with attachment, which is another function that is symbolized by the Moon. In motherhood, we see a tremendous reservoir of emotional content, which is also associated with the Moon.

Attachment can be seen as an unconscious, or conditioned, function of the psyche. Humans do not choose to be attached or detached. They are attached, automatically, due to a web of conditioned feelings, expectations and reflexes. In fact, attachment may be viewed as one of the primary mechanisms by which the Unconscious manipulates and controls the conscious entity, at least while that conscious entity remains not self-actualized and subject to conditioning. To the extent that we are a creature of the collective unconscious rather than an individuated consciousness, our moods, behavior and reactions—all of which are functions associated with the Moon—are largely governed by his/her attachments.

Attachment also plays a vital role within the family for, by and large, family members are bound to each other with very strong karmic attachments. While it is the mother who is primarily symbolized by the Moon, the symbol is generalized to encompass the whole family, acting as a family unit. In this sense, the family is an extension of the mother. The family supports, nurtures, cares for and loves (often in a way that is both unconditional and possessive), just as a mother does. All of these motherly/family functions are functions that are associated with the Moon.

The family function symbolized by the Moon may be further generalized to the idea of "home." Thus, the Moon becomes associated with all things domestic, with the domestic routine, with attachment to home and homeland and with the other emotions associated with one's home. The concept of "home", however, opens another gateway back from the personal dimension of the Moon's symbology to the transcendent dimension.

From the spiritual perspective, this world is not our home and what we consider to be home in this world is nothing more than a way-station, a caravanserai. Our True Home is within, or "further up and further in." [from C.S. Lewis' *The Last* Battle] This direction leads us back toward the Unconscious which, when realized, becomes the super-conscious state. Thus, the Moon, transcendently, symbolizes the function of our seeking for that Real and Eternal state in which we can rest forever—our spiritual Home.

Moving back toward the personal dimension represented by the Moon, there is a strong symbolic association between the Moon and emotion. This is because the subconscious psyche opens out, or back, into what is known as the astral realm, that region of consciousness that immediately transcends the physical world of consensual reality. In this astral realm, there are no physical bodies, but bodies of "light." Without physical bodies, there are no physical sensations, yet "sensation" in this realm is intense. This is the location of various heavens and hells spoken of in most religions. The sensation of the astral realm is all born by emotion. In the physical realm, what is thought of as sensation is a mixture of sense impressions and the feelings invoked by those sense impressions. In the astral realm, it is all feeling.

It is this basic emotional "stuff" of the subconscious, or astral, realm that the Moon symbolizes. This emotional "stuff" is organized or directed by the subconscious and becomes urges, feelings, moods, emotional attachments, etc. These expressions of basic emotion are in constant flux, often repeating themselves cyclically—up and down— just as the Moon continually changes phases. The emotional "stuff" is also very reactive. It is not active or self-determinate, but responds to whatever stimuli it is exposed. Thus, the Moon symbolizes the function of reaction and response.

This emotional "stuff" forms a foundation upon which ordinary, routine life is built. Most people are rooted in this emotional milieu. Even when the emotions are suppressed or not manifested as part of the personality, even when we are not very aware or in touch with our emotions, they are always operating behind the scenes and they are always playing a subconscious role in determining our behavior and responses.

The emotional function that is symbolized by the Moon is generally distinguished from the emotional functions symbolized by Venus, Neptune and, to a certain extent, Mars. These latter are specific and directed in nature, whereas the emotional function symbolized by the Moon is basic—the raw stuff of emotion, emotion that proceeds out of the subconscious and then is manifested in the world of consensual reality in various forms as it is conditioned by the situations within which it is expressed.

Much of what the Moon symbolizes is related to the ordinary, our personal life. Particularly, for those individuals whose consciousness is more or less absorbed in emotion, routine, family and domestic life, the Moon represents the personal dimension of life. However, this may still be true even when we are involved in other, more public or impersonal aspects of life. The individual who is "Moon-dominated" approaches these areas of life from a perspective of personal consciousness. For one who has a more balanced psyche, the Moon may still symbolize that dimension of his/her personality that is personal as opposed to social, societal and/or transcendent. If this is case, then the Moon's symbology is richer, because it opens back out into the subconscious and the intuitive.

The Moon rules the water sign, Cancer. It is strongly associated with the water element. Emotionality is a quality represented by water. The Moon's association with the tides and their rhythmic cycle also strengthens its association with the water element.

The Ascendant

Along with the Sun and the Moon, the Ascendant is generally considered to belong to the trilogy of major astrological symbols. The Ascendant is the first point of the horoscope and begins the progression through the astrological houses. Its symbolic significance is tied to the meaning of the number "One." "One" is the Alpha and the Omega— the Beginning and the End.

Metaphysically, the Alpha is the Omega. "One" is the microcosm and the macrocosm. From the cosmic or metaphysical perspective, all numbers are contained within the number "One."

Given that the Ascendant is the first degree of the astrological chart, this first degree can be seen to contain the entire astrological chart within its essence. It is that point from which the astrological chart proceeds and to which it returns. Because the Ascendant ties together the entire horoscope in this way, it symbolizes the integration of the entire psyche and the personality.

All other points on the astrological chart and, therefore, all planets relate to the Ascendant. The Ascendant symbolically determines the point of view from which we view both our external consensual reality and our internal subjective reality. The Ascendant symbolizes this psychological function of integration, which is like a lens through which we perceive the world and ourselves. Because of its function as a focus for the psyche, the Ascendant plays a major role in the formulation of the personality. This psychological lens or focal point that is symbolized by the Ascendant determines how we view the world. This, in turn influences how we view ourselves and how we views ourselves in the world. All of this is reflected in our personality.

Symbolically linked to the concept of microcosm/macrocosm, the Ascendant also symbolizes the link between our internal psyche (the microcosm) and the role that we play in the world (the macrocosm). More specifically, this relationship between the psyche and the world is the image of the personality that we project into the world—i.e., our persona. Thus, the Ascendant first symbolizes the function of the integration of the psyche, then the formulation of integrated personality and finally the projection of this personality as an image in the world.

This image, or persona, is the person that others see. It is our public personality. This public personality—persona— may be, but usually is not, under the conscious control of the individual. In contrasting the Sun and the Ascendant, it is often said that the Ascendant symbolizes how others see us while the Sun represents how we see ourselves.

Realizing that the persona is not the real self, but only a covering of the self—or a projection of our consciousness—leads us to another function that is symbolized by the Ascendant—the body. For, the body is simply a covering—a projection of the consciousness—at a much grosser material level than that level on which the persona is manifested. Thus, the Ascendant may symbolize our external appearance—i.e., our bodily features, as well as how we project ourselves to others.

The more that we are subject to the conditioning forces of the collective unconsciousness, the more we will identify with our body and our persona. The task of the self-realizing individual is to fully recognize that the body and the persona are both only external garments. We can then consciously pursue the work of self-integration and self-actualization. At its highest symbolic manifestation, the Ascendant returns to its state of Oneness. The individual consciousness is integrated and unified and the self realizes its unity with the Self.

Mercury

Mercury symbolizes the personal, or lower, mind and its function. The function of the personal mind is simply to collect data and transmit this data to the psyche, or consciousness, for evaluation.

The mind, as symbolized by Mercury, does not evaluate the data itself. Thus, it is a "neutral" and "objective" observer. Therefore, Mercury and those signs and houses ruled by Mercury tend to possess the quality of objectivity.

The primary source of data for the mind is the sensory impressions. These exist and flow into the mind's scope of awareness as myriad bits. These bits of data are collected and catalogued, or assembled into logical constructs according to pre-conditioned forms or patterns that the mind recognizes as making sense. There is no actual evaluation of these forms undertaken by the mind at this level; it simply places things into categories and transmits these data-laden categories for further processing.

The second source of data for the mind is the activities of the psyche. The psyche receives the data-bundles transmitted by the mind/nervous system and processes these through judging, evaluation, discrimination, decision-making, etc (a function that is symbolized by Venus). The results are thoughts, which are then carried through the consciousness/brain as part of the functioning of the lower mind. Physically, the lower mind uses neural synapses to carry mental communication through the brain. This is communication, symbolized by Mercury, at its most basic level.

Thoughts are expressed, generally, in words and these words may be communicated externally through speech or writing. This level of communication is also the purview of the lower mind. Words and linguistic structures aid the mind in formulating thoughts into more complex constructs, assembling thoughts together in logical patterns in order to reach conclusions. The logical patterns associated with the lower mind function tend to be governed by internal sets of rules. Strings of thoughts tend to be linked to each other linearly. Thus, Mercury also symbolizes logic (particularly linear logic).

Another function of the lower mind that is linked to thinking is the ability to analyze. The analytical ability is the mind's capacity to break down complex phenomena into basic components and manipulate these components on a symbolic level. Analysis then creates the capacity for these symbolic units to be recombined (synthesis) to form new logical constructs.

The functions that Mercury symbolizes, astrologically, include direct sensory perception, communication—especially verbal communication including language and speech--the nervous system and its operation, the (lower) mind, the brain, the intellect, thought (i.e., logical thought), rationality, analysis and synthesis. Mercury is also associated with objectivity and intellectual curiosity. Speed is also something that is associated with Mercury. The Roman God, Mercury—the Winged Messenger—was known for his speed. This association is primarily related to communication. However, the association with speed also applies to an association with alacrity of thought.

The lower mind is a tool of the psyche that can be employed at various levels of consciousness and for various purposes. At less realized levels of consciousness, the lower mind is an instrument simply for collecting and processing sense impressions. Its patterns and actions are conditioned in order to produce predetermined and predictable results that keep us engrossed in the play of the senses and maintain the belief that the world of consensual reality is the only reality, or at least the only knowable reality.

Because, at this level, the lower mind is essentially reactive and conditioned, it is subject to influences emanating from other functions within the psyche. This is especially true when psychological functions are performing dysfunctionally. The lower mind is also subject to influences from our outer environment that, when combined with negative patterns established in the lower mind or other elements of the psyche, result in distorted, negative and dysfunctional mental reactions.

The key to raising the lower mind to higher vibrations of consciousness is for the self to gain and exercise control over the mind. This involves reversing the process whereby the sense impressions control and dictate the reactions and patterns of the lower mind. To an extent, the mind can be brought under control through disciplined logic or reason. "Reason", thus, gains control over "passion." However, the lower mind is still subject to its own conditionings at this level, in so far as its rational structure has been predetermined through external and internal influences.

In order for the control of the mind by the self to be complete, the mind must transcend itself. The intellect must be used to pierce through the veil of intellect. When the mind goes beyond itself and realizes that it is a servant and not the master of the self, then the liberation of both the mind and the self has begun.

Venus

Although Venus is traditionally associated with relationships (or with "love"), the functional associations symbolized by Venus are much more complex than this. The function of relating is closely entwined with the function of evaluating and Venus' astrological role is as strong in one direction as it is in the other. This can be seen in Venus' dual rulership of Libra and Taurus.

At a basic level, relating and relationship forming are integral to the process of evaluating. In many ways, it may be said that the central role that Venus symbolizes is one of evaluation, with the relationship function growing out of this primary role.

From the standpoint of psychological functioning, Venus symbolizes that function which receives the sense and thought impressions carried by the lower mind (symbolized by Mercury) and which then evaluates each impression. In order to evaluate the Mercurian impressions, the psyche must bring into play numerous relationships.

An evaluation is essentially a comparison, or is based upon a comparison. Phenomena are compared to one another and/or to various standards or continuums of value. Evaluation takes place when a phenomenon is placed in relationship to other phenomena and/or to a scale of value. Thus, the psychological evaluative function that Venus symbolizes is constantly forming virtual relationships. It is natural, then, that these abstract relationships form the psychological wherewithal to enable the psyche to form and grasp relationships within the consensual reality. The concept of relationship manifests both on the impersonal level—through an appreciation of form—and at the interpersonal level, in what is commonly understood by the term "relationship."

Another vector through which the evaluative function is associated with the relationship function is found when we look at the psyche's fundamental motivation to undertake evaluation. Besides the need for such a function in order to organize and make sense of the myriad impressions being delivered to the psyche by the Mercurian function, the primary motivation for the psyche's evaluative activities is to satisfy the ego's need to feel worthy and validated. From the Freudian perspective, the ego wishes to partake in pleasure and to avoid pain. By feeling pleasure, the ego has a sense that it is being rewarded and that, through this reward, its existence is validated. In other words, it is worthy of pleasure. When it feels pain, on the other hand, the ego has a sense of rejection, of punishment and of unworthiness.

The function symbolized by Venus is that which determines what is pleasurable and what is painful, what is to be liked and what is to be disliked. The individual is attracted to that which is pleasurable and to be liked and is repulsed by that which is painful. Similarly, we generally wish to attract to ourselves that which will provide us with pleasure and we desire to repulse that which will cause us pain. Here, then, we have sets of opposing associations that are attached to Venus as an astrological symbol—pleasure/pain, attraction/repulsion, liking/disliking.

These associations not only are integral to the processes and manifestations of evaluation in the world of consensual reality; they are also integral to the processes of forming and maintaining interpersonal relationship. One enters into inter-personal relationships in order to obtain pleasure, validation, appreciation and feelings of self-worth— among other motivations. Those relationships that result in pain are avoided—unless the we have a perverse desire to experience pain, in which case we will be attracted to dysfunctional and negative relationships. We are attracted to those people with whom we hope to form successful relationships and, in turn, we attempt to attract such persons to ourselves in order to form interpersonal relationship(s). The reverse of this process involves detachment or disengagement from others and also encompasses rejection.

In order to sustain the attraction initiated between two relationship partners, various psychological links are formed that provide mutual pleasure for the partners. These include liking the other person and showing this liking through affection. When attraction/ liking/affection is intense, this emotion is labeled "love." Thus, Venus astrologically symbolizes a host of phenomena that are associated with interpersonal relationship, including affection, attraction, preferences and their opposites.

It is with this set of associations that the astrological Venus has the strongest connection with the Roman goddess, Venus. Venus—the goddess—represents romantic love, feminine attraction, physical (feminine) beauty and the anima, in general. Synchronistic with the association of Venus with the feminine is the association of much of what is astrologically symbolized by Venus as feminine. This includes love and affection, beauty and the appreciation of beauty, the arts, passivity and concern about values (particularly compassionate values). Because of Venus' association with the feminine, it also symbolizes the anima and, also, any important women in our life.

Intense relationships—and even those relationships that may be formed for purely practical purposes without much affection— generally require a construct in order that their duration may be prolonged and a degree of "permanence" achieved. These constructs include marriage and various substitutes for marriage. They also include traditional preludes to marriage. When relationships are undertaken for reasons other than affection, these constructs include partnerships and contracts. All of these constructs are astrologically associated with Venus.

The internal evaluative function that is symbolized by Venus manifests in other forms besides interpersonal relationship. People form evaluative judgments about things other than people, some of which are inanimate. In fact, people are constantly evaluating the whole range of sensory experience that is presented to the psyche by the function symbolized by Mercury. The psyche employs the filter of like/dislike and determines whether it should be attracted to or should avoid the sensory stimulus. This function can be generally described by the term, "taste." The psychological function symbolized by Venus is the prime arbiter of "taste." Whether you like or dislike a particular phenomenon, whether you are attracted to it or repulsed by it, is determined by your taste for the phenomenon. Venus, symbolically, is therefore associated with a whole range of psychological functions and attitudes relating to taste.

One major psychological construct used by the psyche to evaluate phenomena relative to taste is the idea of "form." Form is a psychological construct that assembles the Mercurian data into patterns that are meaningful to the psyche. Form refers not only to shape or structure, but to the whole set of qualitative attributes that are attached to something. If the form of something is pleasing—that is, if it accords with your taste—the phenomenon is pleasurable. If the form does not accord with your taste, you are neutral or find it repulsive. Thus, astrologically the Venus-symbol is associated with all aspects of form.

This includes the form-based arts, particularly painting, sculpture, crafts and music.

Another major psychological construct that is used by the psyche to evaluate phenomena is value. Value is an abstract notion of worth and is generally based how attractive something is. The concept of value can be applied to a range of phenomena from the concrete to the abstract. The sum of the values that are possessed by a person constitutes his/her set of values. If a person has formed his/her "set of values", either consciously or unconsciously, into some rational order, this set can then be called a "value system." Venus is astrologically associated with the process of valuation, values and value systems.

In modern society, most people value material goods highly, if not as the paramount objects of value. This is particularly true if they are conditioned by the collective consciousness or society. Given this, Venus has a strong symbolic association, astrologically, with material comfort, material goods and money. Furthermore, society predisposes people to consider material goods as satisfying or enjoyable, not in the abstract or when enjoyed in common, but when these goods become property owned by the individual him/herself. Thus is derived Venus's association—and much of the association of both Taurus and the second house, which are ruled by Venus—with possessions and wealth.

The level of consciousness at which the psychological function symbolized by Venus manifests is largely dependent upon the value system possessed by the individual. At the level of conditioned, unrealized consciousness, the Venus-function reacts to the sensory inputs provided to it by the Mercury-function, being blindly attracted to what is sensually pleasurable and rejecting what is unpleasant to the senses. Our value system, whatever the messages from the super-ego, is based upon our desire to enjoy pleasure and avoid pain, as these are defined by sense experience. We inevitably apply this same strategy to our inter-personal relationships.

This is not to say the sensory enjoyment is wrong or that an ascetic approach to life is correct. However, the realized soul will relegate the goal of acquiring sensory enjoyment to a subordinate position. His/her value system will have been transformed so that it is directed by spiritual vision. That individual will consciously reference his/her value system as he/she goes through life making decisions and evaluating circumstances. To establish a value system at the transcendent level of consciousness, the assistance of the Mercury-function will most likely be needed, so that we may think about our values and rationally consider them. However, it is also likely that some transcendent influence will also be required to accomplish this task. Once a transcendent value system is established, the lower mind again becomes useful in assisting the evaluative function of the psyche to control actions and desires through the exercise of rational discipline.

The support of the mental function is a necessary, but ultimately dispensable, tool. For the core of the self-realized individual's system of values is Love. Within the consciousness of such a person, the concept of Love has evolved from the level of the profane and the sensory to that of the Divine and the Transcendent. As it has done so, Love has, more and more, permeated the individual's consciousness. Love has a selfless quality and is marked by the desire of the lover to please the beloved more than ourselves. As the quality of Love becomes primary in a person's consciousness, we radiate Love for the whole creation—a Love that is grounded in the Love for the Uncreated.

Mars

Mars symbolizes the functional process that naturally follows in the sequence of sense impression reception and communication, evaluation and action. Once formed, the psyche's evaluations become the cause of our taking action. The process through which an evaluative judgment becomes action is symbolized astrologically by Mars.

In order for the psyche to formulate action, its evaluative judgments must first be transformed into desire or motivation. Desire is the result of the attraction created by the Venus-symbolized psychological function. Desire can be seen as that function that activates the formerly passive attraction. The purpose of desire is for us to obtain that to which we are attracted. Desire may be brief and/or related primarily to the execution of an action. Before any action is taken, whether this is reaching for an apple or getting married, there is necessarily a desire to take that action.

Desire assumes a more noticeable and longer-lasting form when the execution of an action must be postponed or when the object of desire cannot be obtained. Desire then takes on a life of its own. It may make deep grooves in the mind, so that the habit of repeated desiring bends the psyche's thoughts toward the object of desire. The person will think about obtaining that object and even about the desire itself. If the desire is intense, we may become "obsessed with our desire." The desire consumes a disproportionate share of our psyche. It monopolizes and colors our thoughts. It colors and clouds our judgment. It may cause us to act in inappropriate ways.

Despite its potential for creating dysfunction in the psyche, desire performs a positive and necessary function. This function is to motivate to action. Without desire, humanity would be goal-less. Without desire, no meaningful action would occur. Desire that is harnessed and focused becomes motivation.

Motivation is not always simple. It is frequently a product of multiple desires. Furthermore, the mental function has often interacted with the desire in various ways. For instance, the lower mind thinks, consciously or automatically, about various desires and assembles them into motivation or a conscious will to take action. The mental function verbalizes our desires so that we can become more aware of them. The mental function is also used to create a pathway whereby motivation is translated into action. The propensity for the mental function symbolized by Mercury and the desire function symbolized by Mars to interact with each other lends a certain quality of objectivity to Mars.

There may also be subconscious influences on the motivation. When this occurs, desire may become "irrational." Because the subconscious is home to a variety of suppressed or unexpressed complexes, such "irrational" desire is not infrequently complex and difficult to scrutinize and disentangle.

Raw desire is generally direct and simple. There may be fiery emotion associated with desire (hence, the expression "burning desire"). One feels desire. Thus, Mars is astrologically associated with the more active forms of emotion. These include lust and anger and their various manifestations (e.g., sexual arousal, irritation, frustration). These also include passion, enthusiasm, eagerness, impulsiveness and aggressiveness. All of these active emotions are expressions of the will to act (or of the will to act being blocked). In fact, the more the will to act is thwarted, the more passionate and violent is the emotional energy associated with the desire function likely to be. The ultimate purpose of highly activated emotional state is to attain the object of desire.

Sometimes, the desire function is so blocked and suppressed that these highly activated emotions begin to take over the psyche. Often, the controlling mental function is weak or absent. We are unable to become aware of our motivations and, so, these play out blindly within the psyche and on the stage of life. The results are most often disastrous for all concerned.

When the desire function operates properly and without intractable resistance, action is the natural result. When there is a conscious awareness of desire, then the motivating link that produces action is termed "will." When the desire function operates automatically to result in action, the motivating link is termed "impulse" or "reaction." Thus, will, impulse and reaction are all associated with Mars.

In some people, there is a predominance of one or the other. Such a predominance will affect our mode of action. People vary in other ways concerning how the person goes about performing action and how he/she goes about getting what he/she wants. The way in which someone acts is a quality of that action. The sign placement of Mars, as well as its aspects and house placement, are all symbolic of our mode of action.

One factor affecting the mode of action is the degree of resistance that we experience to our will and ability to act. Resistance should be distinguished from blockage and suppression, which bring about frustration, in that resistance can be met and overcome with effort. Mars symbolizes this effort to overcome resistance or inertia. Thus, Mars is typically associated with the cardinal or active modality in astrology. When resistance is significant or long lasting, effort becomes determination. Thus, Mars may also symbolize the degree of determination possessed by the individual.

Determination and desire may combine to result in devotion. In fact, devotion may be identified as strong desire combined with the steadfast application of effort in order to fulfill that desire. In devotion, desire, will and action are all intensely focused on a single goal. Through attunement of the individual's value system to the Transcendent or the Divine, that goal becomes the union of the self with the Divine. By devoting oneself to attainment of this highest Goal, the function that is symbolized by Mars achieves its transcendent potential.

The active principle that is symbolized by Mars is traditionally associated with masculine energy. Furthermore, the qualities associated with Mars, the Roman god of war—assertiveness and aggression, taking the offensive, courage and bravery, physical skill and strength, and boldness—are all primarily associated with the masculine. Desire, itself, is an active principle, as opposed to attraction, which operates passively. Mars symbolizes the desirer, whereas Venus can be placed in opposition as the object of desire. Mars is the pursuer, which is traditionally a male role.

Therefore, Mars symbolizes the animus within the psyche. At its basic level, the animus is the hunter, going after the desired prey. Mars, and the animus, also are associated with the male sexual energy, which—traditionally—pursues, conquers, breaches and impregnates. Mars not only symbolizes the masculine energy but also may personify significant male figures in our lives. Typically, such male figures include lovers, leaders and brothers-in-arms.

The masculine principle symbolized by Mars, although sexually oriented for most or many, is subject to transformation. Because the masculine principle is associated with action taken in pursuit of an end, the ultimate desire and goal of the individual will affect his/her concept of masculinity. For most people, masculinity has been defined and conditioned by gender stereotypes. In order to transform the animus, one must break out of these stereotypes. The image of the warrior is useful in illustrating the transformation of which the Mars symbol is capable. At a base level, the warrior seeks booty and the spoils of war—violent triumph, riches and sexual conquest. Acted upon by the super-ego, the individual becomes a "good soldier," doing "what he is supposed to do" to "be a man." When the transcendent goal of spiritual attainment becomes his/her heart's desire, the individual engages in the real *jihad*, the inner struggle for self-liberation and the fight against the *nafs*, or lower tendencies. When we are successful in this struggle, we become a real (hu)man—independent of the collective consciousness and able to stand straight facing the Divine.

Mars is primarily associated with the fire element. Fire is active and liberates energy. The destructive potential of fire is associated with war and aggression, both of which Mars represents. The activity and enthusiasm that Mars can represent are also qualities of the fire element.

Jupiter

It has been noted by others that Jupiter is a transitional planet, forming a bridge between the personal psyche and its functions (represented by the Sun, the Moon, the Ascendant, Mercury, Venus and Mars--the inner planets) and the trans-personal psyche and its transformative functions (represented by Uranus, Neptune and Pluto—the outer planets). As such, the psychological process symbolized by Jupiter is half force and half function. The essence of Jupiter's symbolic meaning can be summed up as Expansiveness.

The quality of expansiveness, however, is a jumping off point for several related qualities and functions that are symbolized by Jupiter. Clearly, Jupiter is associated with outward, expansive motion and with pushing out the boundaries of experience beyond the confines of the personal self. Thus, Jupiter is associated with exploration, with acquiring new experiences and with physical or territorial expansion.

Because expansion is accompanied by an enlargement of scope, Jupiter is also associated with largeness in size. Size is a quality that is not necessarily confined to the physical dimension, although wide girth is a typical Jupiterian trait. Large-sized emotions include enthusiasm, boisterousness, good fellowship and heartiness. Large-sized ideas include broad-mindedness, grand schemes and seeing the big picture. When size is expanded beyond propriety, however, exaggeration and excess occur. These are often defense mechanisms set up by the subconscious to bolster the insecure ego

The functions of exploration and expanding one's experience beyond current horizons suggest another prime function symbolized by Jupiter—that of understanding. Understanding presupposes that the individual has gained a perspective that is "outside" the observed phenomenon. He/she has expanded his/her awareness to the point that he/she can see the entire phenomenon, its internal structure and how it relates to other phenomenon.

Understanding is also accomplished through assimilation. As we expand our experience and awareness, we incorporate what we are acquiring through expansion into our framework of understanding, or worldview. Assimilating experience provides fodder for further growth and expanding horizons. It also adds depth to understanding, because we now "own" the experience which we have acquired, comprehend it and fit it into our worldview. Thus, Jupiter symbolizes understanding, the process of assimilation (and acculturation) and a person's worldview.

The worldview can be seen as a pattern of understanding, or the accumulation of similar ways of understanding reality that coalesce into a whole, single viewpoint. For most people, the worldview is heavily conditioned by society, the super-ego and past experience. The task of the self-realizing soul is to transform his/her worldview, break out of its conditioning and see Reality as it is.

The development of understanding and the transformation of one's worldview results in personal growth. Growth is closely associated with expansiveness. Growth is the intelligent product of expansion (unless the growth is excessive and undisciplined, like kudzu or cancer). Jupiter symbolizes growth, whether this is physical, emotional, psychological or intellectual growth.

Intellectual and spiritual growth and understanding are, generally, not arrived at autonomously, but require and experienced teacher. Therefore, Jupiter symbolizes a mentor or teacher in a person's life. Jupiter may also symbolize the role of being a teacher, imparting understanding or being a role model.

Understanding also presupposes a certain amount of organization and construct. One does not understand chaos; one understands that which has form and relationship. Therefore, the expansiveness symbolized by Jupiter is not the unlimited, infinite expansion that may be associated with Neptune, but a governed and limited expansiveness that occurs within boundaries and according to preestablished rules of order. Jupiter is, therefore, associated with established institutions that promote order in society. The existence of good order enables a cohesive worldview that holds society together to be passed down and assimilated by the members of society. Such institutions include schools and universities, religious institutions and governments.

Positive expansiveness at the emotional level produces good feelings. Emotional outgoingness is generally associated with feelings of good will, generosity and happiness. Therefore, Jupiter is traditionally associated with these positive emotional states. Expansiveness at the material level results in abundance. This is another trait that is typically associated with Jupiter. Material abundance and emotional good will result in feelings of liberality and generosity, both Jupiterian traits. Liberality, when combined with understanding and an expansive outlook produces broadmindedness. Thus, Jupiter is generally seen as symbolizing beneficence in all its forms. This has been the cause of the common perception of Jupiter as a "favorable" planet. It is often pointed out, however, that too much "good luck" and ease can be detrimental to character development. It can not only remove growth-producing stress, but also lead to complacency, laziness and a selfish attitude.

The concepts of liberality and beneficence, when manifested at the transcendent or spiritual level, are linked to the idea of grace. Grace can be defined as that liberal quality of Spirit that results in "free gift." Spiritually, these gifts are the virtues, particularly Love, spiritual understanding, devotion and being kept on the "straight path." These gifts naturally generate gratitude toward the Giver. This state of gratitude and humility produces qualities of sweetness, gentleness, generosity and high-mindedness in the recipient of grace. Thus, grace leads to gracefulness. It also produces true ease of mind, since the recipient of Divine Grace knows that he/she must rely on the Giver of that grace and not on his/her own ego- and desire-motivated efforts. At its transcendent potential, therefore, Jupiter symbolizes spiritual grace and the Giver of the Divine Gift, as well.

Saturn

Saturn is Jupiter's opposite as a transitional planet. It represents restriction and limitation as opposed to Jupiter's expansiveness. Where Jupiter is associated with abundance and happiness, Saturn is often associated with hardship and pain. While Jupiter is associated with liberality, Saturn represents exactingness and harsh adherence to the law. Both Jupiter and Saturn, however, represent functions that are based in the preservation of order and the maintenance of the world-as-it-is.

Saturn is traditionally seen as a "malefic" planet in the old school of astrology. It is true that Saturn symbolizes that entity or psychological function named Satan, Shaytan and Kal in the Christian, Islamic and Hindu-Sikh traditions. What is lost sight of is the positive function that is exercised in this setting up of a negative pole within the consciousness. In certain Sufi traditions, Shaytan is said to the most dutiful servant of Allah. In the Hindu-Sikh tradition, Kal was given rulership of the "three worlds" after performing ascetic devotions for millions of years.

The Greek name for Saturn is Cronus and Saturn is, indeed, intimately associated with time. Kal means time. Time is the complicating dimension of the time-space continuum. Jupiter's expansiveness is related to space and Saturn's time dimension stands in oppositional relationship to Jupiter's expansive space. It is the finiteness of time that ultimately limits the expansion of space. Saturn's association with time also makes it a symbol of old age and—the end of time as we know it—death. Both are "unpleasant" subjects to most people.

Death places the ultimate bounds or limits on human life. This, then, is one way in which the Saturnian association with limitation is derived. Again, the association is not pleasant in most people's minds. Limitation, itself, is a thorn in the side of the ego, for the ego secretly desires to be infinite and all-powerful. It chafes under the idea that it is finite and limited, as represented by Saturn.

Saturn's association with the "finality" of death also evokes another important meaning of Saturn—judgment. This is as in "Judgment Day." Saturn represents the archetype of the Judge of Good and Bad Deeds. It is the entity/function represented by Saturn who, in the traditional religions, assigns souls to reward in Heaven or punishment in Hell. This secret--that the Divine lies beyond Saturn's realm of time and space, beyond the concepts of Good and Evil, reward and punishment—is essential to understanding the key function and essence of the Saturn symbol. The primary function symbolized by Saturn is that of Gatekeeper. Saturn does not let any soul pass into the Timelessness and Infinity of Eternity unless it is completely Pure and unattached to anything in the material creation.

Thus, Saturn acts as a divine filter. The "wheels of Time grind exceedingly slowly, but exceedingly fine." "Not a grain that blows into your field from your neighbor's granary" escapes Saturn's demand for payment. It is such harsh exactitude that throws most of us back into the "darkness where there will be much weeping and gnashing of teeth." Is it any wonder that Saturn is perceived in such a bad light?

One of the positive qualities represented by Saturn is that through its exact demandingness, purification is achieved. The Saturn function, acting through the subconscious and the collective mind, presents the individual with a series of life lessons and challenges—tests which he/she must pass in order to demonstrate his/her character or learning experiences that will ultimately result in gaining greater understanding and higher consciousness.

From a karmic perspective, Saturn represents the principle that the consequences of every action performed by an individual must be experienced by that individual, usually in some future life. Saturn signifies such consequence, particularly when the consequence is for a negative action (consequences of positive actions tend to be associated with Jupiter or the Part of Fortune). Consequences of negative actions tend to be in the form of experiences that are designed to purify, deter from future negative action or redeem the individual. They are generally perceived by most people as punishment, bad luck or misfortune, however.

The road leading to spiritual purification is not a super-highway. It is a lifetime's work and, if one believes in reincarnation, then it can be said that it is the work of a great many lifetimes. The lessons that the Saturn function brings are, therefore, likely to be incremental. This generally means that they are repetitive and subtle, designed to bring a person to change gradually over an extended period of time. Much of the intended result of the Saturnian lessons is to strengthen will and discipline and instill the other "strong" virtues. In other words, most people are still in the early stages of being prepared to meet spiritual tests and they are a long way off from any spiritual achievement. The slow and steady pace at which this process takes place is a quality that is associated with Saturn.

Nevertheless, there are certain qualities that must be instilled in the individual if he/she is to progress spiritually. These include discipline, persistence, patience and strength of will. Not everyone develops these virtues and many, rather than progressing forward, retrograde when faced with Saturn's tests. The Saturnian virtues are often instilled through the meeting of obstacles, limitations, hardships and challenges. Meeting these circumstances builds character or exposes weaknesses in character. Such difficult circumstances, with which Saturn is often identified, are rarely popular with those upon whom they befall.

Successfully facing these circumstances requires structure and organization, besides the virtues described above. This is another side of the Saturn symbol. For Saturn is not only the Gatekeeper, but ultimately the "ruler" of the material worlds. It is the Saturnian principle that structures the material creation and allows it to manifest concretely. The manifestation of the material, from a metaphysical perspective (and, considering the implications of $E=MC^2$, from a scientific perspective, as well), is a crystallization of subtle energy. The farther consciousness descends onto the physical plane, the denser and harder materiality becomes. These properties of concreteness, crystallization, rigidity and hardness are all qualities that are associated with Saturn.

The material world is not chaos. Everywhere we look, the mind produces form and structure. From the microscopic to the cosmic, form and structure pervade everywhere. Form and structure presuppose rule and law. Karmic consequence also presupposes that there are cosmic or natural laws that can be "violated" to generate negative consequences or abided by to earn reward. Rules, order, law and authority are all phenomena that are symbolized by Saturn. Saturn also has a natural association with the super-ego—the internal enforcer of collective/societal rules and mores--as is suggested by the fact that the natural Midheaven occurs at the first degree of Saturn-ruled Capricorn.

The structure, organization and order that Saturn symbolizes is a function of Reason. Reason is used here in the sense that it was used during the Enlightenment. It is the structuring or governing Principle. However, Saturn also symbolizes the side of Reason that is seen in Blake's Urizen—that portion of the psyche that is bound by its own rules and constructs and is, like Satan, permanently shut off from the Transcendent Reality that is above all mind and illusion.

It is ironic that Saturn is not only the Cosmic Judge and Jailer who keeps souls imprisoned in the material worlds (which includes the heavens and hells) and is also the Cosmic Strengthener, demanding that the conscious being follow the "straight path," become freed of all impurities and offering cosmic isometric resistance to the soul. It is the individual's task to enlist the aid of this harshest of cosmic taskmasters so that, ultimately, he/she is capable of walking through the Single Gate into Infinity.

Saturn is most closely associated with the earth element. Earth is solid and stable, like those structures associated with Saturn. In the physical realm, structures are traditionally built out of earth or rock. Earth represents enduringness and resistance to change.

Uranus

Uranus is the first of the outer, or transformative planets. The function of the three outer planets is to break down, in one way or another, the rigid perception of reality in which the consciousness has been trapped. The ultimate goal of these functions is to liberate the individual from the limited reality that is symbolized by the personal planets, Jupiter and especially Saturn.

It has often been said that Saturn represents a rigidification of the structure and worldview that were originally necessary to provide the psyche with the tools necessary to function effectively in the consensual reality. Over time, however, as the psyche matures and develops potential for further growth, these constructs become outmoded and detrimental. Thus, the goal of the functions symbolized by the outer planets has been said to be to break down, by various means, these rigid structures and allow the psyche to move into a new and more consciously aware phase of growth and development.

Another way in which to view these outer planet functions is that they are transformative. The worldview and habitual, conditioned way of life and thought that are symbolized by Jupiter and Saturn are, in most people, so fixed, so entrenched that to dislodge these crystallized concepts from the psyche requires a total change. These crystallized constructs may be seen as "dead" forms. The processes of transformation that are symbolized by the outer planets can be seen as analogous to rebirth, in the spiritual sense of this term. Thus, the outer planets bring new life to the moribund consciousness. They free it from the prison of its own making—the prison of crystallized forms and attachments to the way things are.

The transformative function symbolized by Uranus acts by introducing change. Truly transformative change must originate from outside the framework symbolized by Saturn, Jupiter and the inner planets. All of the aforementioned functions, unless operating at their transcendent (i.e. transformed) potentials, are operating at the level of the consensual reality—the material world. They are conditioned by the Collective Unconscious.

The transformative change introduced by the Uranus function proceeds from the Higher Mind. Uranus, the Greek god, was the personification of the heavens, symbolizing higher consciousness. The

Higher Mind may be defined as that element of the Universal Mind that draws the personal mind (or lower mind) upward toward higher levels of consciousness. It is a part of the Collective Unconscious, but it is that part that seeks to liberate the psyche from its conditioning rather than bind the psyche through conditioning. In a sense, the Higher Mind is the Collective Unconscious made conscious, or at least in the process of becoming conscious. Thus, Uranus is often portrayed as the higher octave of Mercury.

Because the personal mind is, initially, not conscious of the Higher Mind, the Higher Mind must have some vehicle with which to communicate with the lower mind. Words are a part of the consensual reality, symbolizing reality in commonly agreed upon images and meanings. Words and all other traditional forms of communication are not sufficient for the use of the Higher Mind, although the Higher Mind may make use of them. The vehicle that must be used by the Higher Mind is revelation.

In order for revelation to be received by the psyche, the psyche must possess a certain degree of receptivity or attunement. The psyche's receptivity may not be apparent; it may be latent. This is the case when revelation and insight come to the individual "out of the blue," as it were. Revelation descends upon the individual. Then, "flash! Paradise!" [Jefferson Airplane in She Has Funny Cars] At other times, revelation may crash upon the individual. Such revelation is powerful and generally results in a sudden transformation of the psyche's outlook and perceptions.

When revelation comes suddenly upon the psyche, it is not because of the autonomous or arbitrary force of the Higher Mind, but because we have subconsciously arrived at that point where our conscious mind is ready and receptive to such a revelation. The effect that revelation may have upon the psyche, whether temporary or more permanent, cannot be predicted, but is a function of our spiritual maturity and "good karma." It must follow that not everyone is at the point of receptivity to the transformative energy symbolized by Uranus.

When a change in our psyche is firmly established and when we have digested the revelation that we have received from the Higher Mind, we may develop an attunement to the forces of the Higher Mind. This opens another channel of communication between the Higher Mind and the personal mind—that of intuition. Intuition in its pure form is a vehicle whereby revelation from the Higher Mind may be received in a more stable, gentler fashion.

Through intuition, the individual becomes acclimated to the realm of the Higher Mind. Those principles that are true and eternal from a cosmic or macrocosmic perspective begin to permeate our psyche. We begin to replace those conditioned behaviors, outlooks and reactions that we had formerly held with behavior that is based upon true insight. We see that, in Reality, all is One and this knowledge informs his/her actions and attitudes. Acting from our own enlightened self-interest, we exercise compassion and wish to improve the conditions of others. Thus, Uranus is associated with altruism and humanitarian actions.

Society, however, is firmly organized around the principles indoctrinated by the Collective Unconscious as symbolized by Saturn and Jupiter. The condition of the world is a result of those principles and the ways in which individual egos relate to and use these principles. Any real improvement in the lot of humanity, therefore, requires that the very principles upon which the world functions be altered and replaced with principles that are derived from a higher Truth. Such fundamental change in the way in which society operates is termed "revolution" or "radicalism" by the established Jupiter/Saturn-based institutions that hold society together. Thus, Uranus is also identified with political revolution and social causes of all types.

The revolutionary aspect of Uranus is even more fundamental than this, however. The forces symbolized by Uranus seek to utterly replace the old constructs symbolized by Saturn with new constructs that are derived from the Higher Mind. In order to accomplish this, the old constructs must be swept away. It is not a question of incrementalism. Incrementalism is a Jupiterian means of change. It occurs within and as a part of the established order. Uranus symbolizes radical change.

One of the most radical and—to the old order—subversive type of change is the liberation of the psyche from the constraints of the Collective Unconscious. Jung called this process "individuation." The individuation of the psyche occurs when it recognizes that it is not that which is defined by the collective and proceeds to discover its own real self-identity. Thus, it is a process of both de-conditioning and discovery. As the psyche detaches itself from the conditionings of the

Collective Unconscious, it discovers its own uniqueness as a singular microcosm within and united to the macrocosm. Ultimately, it becomes the One—but a one that is also one of the unique expressions of the Infinite.

As the individual becomes detached from and less a captive of the Collective Unconscious, he/she begins to differentiate him/herself from the collective. He/she is no longer defined by the collective. He/she is no longer an anonymous nonentity conforming to the mass consciousness. He/she begins to see him/herself as an individual. As an individual, he/she wishes to distinguish him/herself (or is automatically distinguished) from the collective. He/she takes on non-conformist characteristics and behaviors. To the extent that the person is still bound by his/her ego, these non-conformities may be more or less self-conscious. Nevertheless, they are often the first stirrings of the individuation process. Thus, Uranus is closely identified with unconventional behavior and with individuation.

As mentioned above, there is a danger that unconventional behavior will substitute for the real work of individuation. In this way, the ego remains untransformed. Rather than living in the Truth that has been revealed by the Higher Mind, we still reference ourselves to the illusion represented by the consensual reality. In fact, the ego and the conditioning part of the subconscious devise a variety of ways to thwart the transformative power symbolized by Uranus.

Most often, the transformative urge to completely change and replace the old and outmoded constructs to which the psyche is attached is channeled into "safe" modes. These safe modes allow the function symbolized by Uranus some outlet. The idea that any real change may be taking place, however, is an illusion.

One of these safe modes involves a partial differentiation from the collective. The process of individuation is taken only so far. Usually, this involves the identification of the individual with some group. The group, whether it is a club or a social movement, provides some level of differentiation from the mass collective for the individual. It gives us a sense of uniqueness without having to bear the painful loneliness of real uniqueness. Thus, Uranus (and the eleventh house which it rules) has come to be associated with groups and peer organizations of all kinds.

Individualism, as opposed to individuation, is another half-measure that is identified with Uranus. Here, the psyche clings to the ego and the persona and assumes that it is these entities, rather than the self, that are unique. In actuality, at the ego/persona level, a person is basically like everyone else. The denial of this commonality and the urge to see ourselves as unique individuals often push a person to extremes of individualism. Because this individualism is ego-based, there is often a resistance to feelings of social responsibility and humanitarianism with which Uranus is otherwise associated.

Change is another suboptimization of the transformative function symbolized by Uranus. The substitution of change for transformation can take place internally or it can manifest externally. If the substitution is made internally, then we will find ourselves attracted to change or, more accurately, rearrangement. Change may be pursued for changes sake or a goal may be adopted that focuses on change. Such a goal may be mundane—such as changing your partner—or noble—such as changing the world. In either case, change is employed as a distraction from the real task at hand, which is the transformation of the self through radical constitutional change within the psyche. As John Lennon put it, "You better change your mind instead." [Revolution]

The more the transformative energy symbolized by Uranus presses upon the insecure ego, the more desperate the ego becomes to defend itself. Frivolous change (from the viewpoint of the Higher Mind) is latched onto by the ego even to the point of this being detrimental to the health of the psyche and the persona. The attempts of the ego to ward off transformation by substituting change can result in instability, unreliability, eccentricity and erratic behavior in the individual. Nervousness and worry over change can also be symptoms of the ego's defensiveness.

Especially if our other character traits tend toward stability and a conservative personality, the subconscious mind may externalize change in its attempt to preserve the insecure ego. In these cases, Uranus symbolizes the experience of change by us. Often, such change is sudden and unexpected. Often, too, it is viewed by the individual as destructive or, at least, disruptive.

The Collective Unconscious possesses one great, last defense if the transformation brought about by the Higher Mind is not total and self-transformative. This phenomenon is symbolized in Greek legend by Cronus' overthrow of Uranus. Cronus was Uranus' son and his overthrowing his father symbolizes the phenomenon of that which emanates from the inspiration and new vision of Uranus eventually becomes old, rigidified and a part of the status quo. Then, it is no longer Uranian, but Saturnian, and the outpouring of transformative energy from its source in the Higher Mind must begin again, or take a new tact.

Uranus is most closely associated with the air element, as is its sub-octave, Mercury, but more ambiguously. Sky and the heavens, which are associated with Uranus, are of the air. The transparency of air, its ability to act as a medium for sound transmission (communication) and its natural sharpness and clarity all can be associated with the Uranian function of transmitting the content of the Higher Mind to the psyche.

Neptune

The transformative change symbolized by Uranus is brought down from the Higher Mind and must operate at the level of the consensual reality. The ultimate transformative goal, however, is to move beyond consensual reality. It is Neptune that symbolizes the transformative urge to transcend the material plane of consciousness. Neptune is associated with two related principles—boundarilessness and dissolution. Boundarilessness is the quality represented by Neptune; dissolution is its transformative methodology to reach its goal, which is self-transcendence.

Boundarilessness represents the transcendental state of Infinity and Eternity—the states of being beyond space and time. It is the condition of total absorption and union with the One. Kabir and other mystics have said: "In Love, there is only One. The lane of Love is narrow; it will not let two pass." In the mystical experience, the lover merges her/his identity into the Beloved. As with Hallaj and Bayasid Bizami, there is no longer an "I", there is only "Allah." Therefore "I am the Truth!" is the ecstatic cry. It is Neptune that symbolizes the mystical experience and the psyche's yearning for that union with the Beloved.

Neptune symbolizes the achievement of this mystic experience through *fana*, or the fading away of the ego. There is no violence in this method—no sudden jolt as with Uranian transformation. Rather, the ego loosens its attachments to the material world so that they drop off and dissolve away. The last attachment to dissolve is that of the ego to its own supposed existence and when this occurs, the Real Self is liberated from the bondage of the illusory ego-separation. The Real Self realizes that "All is Illusion"—this "all" referring to the Creation and especially to the material world. This is the process of Neptunian transformation.

The dissolving energy associated with Neptune can operate at a less ultimate level, also. In fact, any construct symbolized by Saturn is susceptible to the disintegrative power represented by Neptune. This force seeks to dissolve away hard and rigid structures and forms. Because of Neptune's association with the disintegration of form, it has sometimes been considered to be a "malefic" planet in traditional astrology, since disintegration disturbs the natural order and causes pain to those who are attached to that order.

The action of this force is in many ways like that of the ocean. The constant action of wave, current and/or salt on solid rock eventually wears away and dissolves the shoreline edifice. Neptune, in Roman mythology, is the god of the sea. The constant and gradual wearing away of the rocky shore (Saturn) by the sea (Neptune) often results in the undermining of a shoreline bluff until, with nothing to support it, it collapses of its own weight.

This erosion of the supporting understructure symbolizes a number of Neptunian phenomena and qualities. It can symbolize an erosion of faith in what was formerly thought to be well established. Skepticism and doubt are primarily Neptunian qualities. Subversiveness is another Neptunian phenomenon that is symbolized by this image. Also, since the Neptunian force is working from the bottom and almost imperceptibly, Neptune may also be a symbol of the subconscious, particularly when it is acting to subvert or undermine the conscious ego.

The ocean image that Neptune symbolizes is also associated with emotion, which is "watery" in nature. The Neptunian emotions, however, are at the opposite pole from the basic emotions represented by the Moon. Neptune is traditionally associated with subtle or fine emotions. At the level of the lower mind, these emotions appear to be vague and ill-defined—a quality associated with Neptune's boundarilessness. These are feelings, intuitions, sensitivities and sixth sense emotions. When manifested negatively, however, these subtle emotions become fears (especially vague and generalized fear), anxiety and neurosis. At the transcendent level, Neptune expresses itself as emotion in ecstasy, spiritual yearning and love—all of which are consummated by merging into the Ocean of Being and Love.

In reality, the transcendent level associated with Neptune is accessible only to a few. While this side of the Neptunian function may manifest for a larger number of people as religious experience, for most people there is an inability to connect to the real Neptunian essence. Therefore, it is common for the psyche to gravitate toward the counter-image of Neptunian transcendence--illusion. Thus, Neptune can represent both sides of the duality of Truth and illusion.

Through its association with illusion, Neptune symbolizes a host of phenomena and qualities, both positive and negative. These include mystery and the mysterious, deception and self-deception, fantasy, imagination, mental illness and escapism. Illusion, when carried to the extreme, is, however, another tool for the suppressed Neptunian function of self-transcendence to dissolve the rigid and established structures that may be holding the native back and entrapping the psyche in the prison of the material world. For, illusion weakens and dissolves the psyche's perception and belief in the consensual reality (which is itself an illusion). If illusion's grasp on us is intense enough, we may "hit bottom" and realize that we have been living an illusion. At this point, a window opens through which we may grasp the existence of a transcendent Reality.

Another suboptimization of the function represented by Neptune involves its goal of self-transcendence. Self-transcendence means that the ego must be abandoned. The idea of the "death" of the ego is sometimes distorted by that part of the subconscious mind that is committed to preserving the ego at all costs. In this distortion, self-transcendence becomes self-destruction. In a bizarre perversion of the Mind, the individual's life is sacrificed so that his/her ego may continue to exist in some wretched form within the confines of the material creation. Typically, the self-destructive tendencies associated with Neptune are associated with extreme indulgence in illusion—substance abuse and addiction, insanity, blind pursuit of a fantasy, martyrdom and becoming a victim, destructive co-dependency and—the ultimate in self-destruction—suicide.

The self-destruction of the individual affects not only him/herself, but also others. The psyche no longer expresses itself as a coherent personality. The person "disappears." Thus, Neptune has become associated with loss and the pain of grief. All of these manifestations, however, are only distorted copies of the positive and transcendent qualities that the transformed self possesses—*fana*, spiritual yearning and the union of the self with the All in All.

Pluto

If the ego is unwilling to undergo transformation through the revelation symbolized by Uranus or the transcendent pull symbolized by Neptune, it may have to suffer the crises symbolized by Pluto. The ultimate goal symbolized by Neptune and Pluto are actually the same— the union of the self with the One Being. It can be said, however, that in most cases the way represented by Pluto is more difficult. That there are two paths that lead to the same conclusion is symbolized by the astronomical phenomenon that the orbit of Pluto, at some point, crosses the orbit of Neptune so that Neptune becomes the most outer planet of the solar system.

There is also a "difference" in directionality symbolized by Pluto when compared to Neptune. Neptune can be said to symbolize a movement of the psyche which is "upward and inward" and "dissipating"—upward in the sense that the transcendent exists at a higher level of consciousness than the concrete; upward and dissipating as in the image of water evaporating from a muddy puddle. Pluto, on the other hand, may be said to symbolize a movement of the psyche which is "downward and inward" and "concentrating"—downward in the sense of the journey to the Source deep within the subconscious mind and concentrating as in the image of a reverse Big Bang shedding all extraneous form and structure until it is a uniform singularity.

The function represented by Pluto achieves this uniform singularity—the merging of the consciousness in its Source—through a process of polarization, crisis and a resolution of the crisis through purging. The Plutonian function acts on established, but outmoded, forms first by dividing the phenomenon into its positive and negative poles. It then intensifies the duality of the extremes until a crisis is produced. Pluto's association with the most intense form of duality casts it as a symbol of extremes, as well as intensity.

Since the extreme positive pole represented by Pluto is beyond the scope of most people, Pluto has most often been associated with the negative extreme. Thus, Pluto is often classed as a "malefic" planet in traditional astrology. Pluto is seen to represent evil, the dark side, and to be the cause of much pain and suffering.

It is true that the polarization function symbolized by Pluto defines the "dark side" of the subconscious. Some have said that this is a critical function, since it allows the conscious mind to confront and accept the "irrational" forces of the subconscious, which the conscious mind suppresses and demonizes. Robert Bly has called this "dark" subconscious energy the "Red Man" within each of us (particularly males). The female counterpart to the "Red Man" also exists in a Medusa-like "Wild Woman." Bly and others argue that when these untamed energies are suppressed, psychic fracture results, creating dysfunction and a personality that is not whole and in touch with itself.

The suppressed subconscious forces are also likely to seek manifestation either by "hijacking" the conscious mind or by externalizing the dark side. In the former case, the individual will act "irrationally" and out of character, being motivated by strong and deep subconscious impulses that are not clearly understood. Or, the individual may find him/herself consumed by such basic urges as those for sex or power. These strong, subconscious or basic drives—particularly sex and power—are closely identified with Pluto.

When the suppressed drives are externalized, the Plutonian content is likely to be experienced by the individual as a force that is directed against him/her. This force may be manifested as a person or as an institution, but we are likely to experience it/him/her as powerful, oppressive, controlling, opposed to our will and—often—evil. Because these subconscious forces are generally more powerful than the individual consciousness, we often find ourselves in the position of the victim, the oppressed or the slave in reference to the Plutonian manifestation.

The polarization associated with Pluto, unless it is totally suppressed, will bring about some form of crisis. The purpose of such a crisis is to bring about a resolution of the duality that the Plutonian function has created. The form of the crisis often involves conflict between the two opposites. This conflict may be internal or external, depending upon how the Plutonian energy has been manifested.

If the conflict is externalized, there is a tendency for the person undergoing a Plutonian crisis will see him/herself as the "white knight" or "virgin" opposed by or endangered by the dark forces of evil. When this occurs, the Plutonian function is being played out by proxy and it is rare for any consciousness-based resolution of the crisis to take place. There may be lessons that are being learned by the psyche through its experience of conflict and the various roles that the conscious self may seek to play in dealing with the external crisis.

However, because the crisis is not being dealt with on a conscious level, there is a high risk of failure to learn the lesson at hand and resolve the crisis, with the result that the crisis will have to be repeated in some form or another until some breakthrough occurs— perhaps in this lifetime, perhaps not. In these cases, the end result of the crisis may be damaging to us and involve destruction, loss of power or even death. Pluto has, thus, come to symbolize conflict and oppression, particularly when these have a bad end.

Often the intense pressure that is produced by the Plutonian crisis, whether external or internal, results in an explosion of emotional force. Pluto is symbolic of explosiveness and, in particular, nuclear explosion. In fact, the process of polarization producing crisis and explosion is similar to the nuclear fission process that produces the atomic bomb. The rapid collapse of opposites into their essential unity is symbolized by the process of nuclear fusion. It is a symbolic synchronicity that a key ingredient to a nuclear reaction is the element, Plutonium.

If the conflict is psychological and internalized, we may or may not be prepared to deal with it consciously. Again, there is a tendency for the individual to identify with the "positive" pole of the duality and experience the negative pole as a psychological disruption or problem. If this is the case, the crisis produced may range from a more or less predictable transitional crisis (e.g., mid-life) to the flare up of a neurosis or a psychotic episode. The crisis may also be a spiritual or existential crisis.

If the crisis is to be successfully dealt with, we must first realize that the negativity that we are experiencing comes from our own psyche. We must take ownership of our muck before we can dispose of it. Only then can we deal with the Plutonian crisis at the conscious level.

Sometimes, the internal Plutonian crisis is brought about by an external event. Such an event is often a catastrophic loss, the destruction of something or some construct to which one is attached, or a death. Pluto is associated with destruction and death—associations that only increase its "malefic" reputation. However, it is death and destruction that symbolize the resolution of the Plutonian crisis. For, in order for the crisis of duality to be resolved, the old attachments of the psyche must die. The negativity that has been brought to light by the crisis must be destroyed and purged from the psyche.

This process of destruction and death is, one might imagine, not pleasant to deal with. This is not a gentle loosening of attachment but a cutting or a ripping away of what has become calcified. Another metaphor for the process of Plutonian cleansing is that of the base metal that is melted in the fire to purge it of its impurities. In this case, the fire is the fire of intense psychological crisis and unrelenting confrontation with the truth about ourselves.

The productive, internal crisis that is associated with the Pluto is resolved through a ruthless casting out of the false. As this occurs and the psyche is purified of the dross that it has collected over a long period of time (or lifetimes), the psyche is attracted more and more to the Truth that resides at its core. This Truth is the Source of All Being. This natural attraction of the psyche to its central core, when acted upon by the Plutonian transformative processes, results in the association of Pluto with a host of related phenomena and meanings.

Among these are integrity (which is a hallmark of truth), clear insight (which is a quality of resulting from approaching the Truth and the Source) and the subconscious (which is the road to the Inner Source). The role of the subconscious in creating the circumstances of Plutonian crises has been mentioned previously. Pluto also represents the subconscious as an entity or realm to be delved into and explored— made conscious by the self.

Because this process of self-discovery through the discovery (or exposure) of the subconscious is an inner process, Pluto is also associated with secrecy. Because dealing with the subconscious is not often straightforward, Pluto is also often associated with intrigue. Both of these qualities may manifest in their more negative forms, but both have positive roles to play, as well. Intrigue becomes the inner game of

Love that is played between the self and that Inner Power. Secrecy becomes spiritual intimacy, during which the Secret of Secrets is revealed to the self.

That Inner Power which is at the source of all things is the real Power, of which mundane power is only a shadow. The psyche's yearning for that Source and that Power is reflected in a need for emotional security. Union with that Inner Source provides the greatest feeling of security and safety from all possible dangers and threats. However, before this inner security can be felt, the psyche must expose itself to the power that the Plutonian function brings to bear against the negative and outmoded constructs to which the ego is attached. This creates a heightened state of insecurity, which must be resolved inwardly before the self can seek the safety of its own Source.

The North Node

We return to the major astrological calculated points. The Ascendant was discussed earlier, because of the important psychological functions that it symbolizes. The remaining calculated points are the Moon's Nodes, the Part of Fortune and the Midheaven,.

The Moon's North Node represents the psyche's yearning for its destiny. Thus, it is associated with forward motion, development and the future. It is often said that the North Node points to the destiny of the astrological native. It may, therefore, symbolize that destiny. This is not necessarily the case, however. The Moon's North Node may symbolize a feeling for one's destiny or a desire for a particular destiny. It may also symbolize potential destiny.

As potential destiny, the North Node symbolizes that toward which the individual needs to move and, therefore, that which he/she needs to develop. Thus, the North Node may actually symbolize an area of weakness for the individual. As potential destiny, it is something that he/she needs to expend effort on in order to develop. It is likely to be "new territory" that may be difficult to blaze. Once the ground is broken, however, there may be a natural and magnetic attraction or an irresistible pull to meet and actualize the destiny that is symbolized by the North Node.

A planet conjuncting the North Node is likely to strengthen its significance for the psyche. This may also symbolize that the function represented by that planet needs to be strengthened and developed. Or, it may symbolize that the function is to play some other role in the realization of the individual's destiny.

The transcendent dimension of the North Node points in a single direction—towards spiritual growth and development. This is often the most difficult course of destiny to follow. However, it is almost always rewarding and it has the potential to become that Ultimate Destiny from which there is no return.

The South Node

The Moon's South Node represents the predispositions or innate qualities possessed by the psyche and the personality. It is connected with subconscious memory and with the past. It is often said that the South Node represents our talents and resources. The South Node can be seen to represent not only what is innate and available to us, but also what we are responsible to bring forth and utilize for the benefit of ourselves and others.

One can say that these are the things that the psyche brings with it from its past life experiences. Those skills that the psyche had learned and developed previously are carried forward into this life and are innately instilled in the psyche ready to be reawakened and utilized. Those rewards that have been earned in the past are now reaped and can be drawn upon. Or, one could say that these talents are simply implanted within the psyche or become innate by some other means and that the resources available to the individual are allotted or are a matter of the luck of the draw.

The predispositions symbolized by the South Node also include those conditioned behaviors and habits that seem to be second nature in the individual. One can conceive of these behavior patterns as resulting from the experience and conditioning of previous lifetimes or as resulting from the conditioning received in early childhood. Very often, these habits and behaviors are grounded in psychological complexes to which the individual is attached.

These predispositions may be helpful to the individual or they may hold him/her back. Particularly if there is a planet conjuncting the South Node, there may be some negative and outmoded behavior or psychological pattern that we must overcome and let go if we are to reach our full potential. The nature of the negative attachment is generally symbolized by the conjuncting planet. It has been said that if we hold onto these negative complexes, they have the potential to drag us into a vicious cycle of negativity.

The transcendent potential of the South Node lies in the psyche's innate attraction to its spiritual Source and its innate ability to actualize its real selfhood. There is a saying, "O Bikha! Everyone has jewels in his bundle, but few know how to untie the knot." These spiritual jewels are the innate birthright of all, but most trade them for a mess of pottage. The transcendent South Node points to your ability to untie the knot of the mind and the soul and liberate the psyche from its age-old conditioning.

Part of Fortune

The Part of Fortune, as its name implies, is generally seen as symbolizing the astrological native's good fortune and where he/she can find it. If the Part of Fortune is heavily afflicted, however, this is generally interpreted as the absence of good fortune or the occurrence of bad luck. However, "what is sweet now turns so sour" [The Beatles from Savoy Truffle] and what may appear to be ill fortune may, in time, prove to be the proverbial blessing in disguise.

It should be said that the Part of Fortune symbolizes, not necessarily the good fortune that will come to you, but the potential for good fortune. Although it may signify good (or bad) fortune that comes as a gift, the value of the Part of Fortune is that it signifies what must be done in order to find your good fortune. What that fortune might be is, to a large extent, dependent on what you are seeking, although its nature may also be indicated by the Part of Fortune. The wise will not be fooled by the promise of material fortune or fame but will seek a more mature manifestation of good fortune.

The Part of Fortune may symbolize good fortune that comes easily, though this is not always the case. Some may toil and strive after their good fortune all through life. Some may never find it. Some may be deceived by it. Only a few will recognize and pursue the greatest good fortune, which is self-transcendence.

Midheaven

The Midheaven symbolizes the super-ego. In the natural horoscope, it is the first degree of Capricorn, which is associated with ambition and accomplishment—both of which are values that are prized by the Western super-ego. The Midheaven is also the zenith of the horoscope, which symbolizes a position of power and authority and, also, a goal to be reached—qualities, again, associated with the Western super-ego.

Here, the super-ego is defined as having both a personal component and an impersonal component. Thus, our definition of the super-ego does not necessarily conform to the psychological theoretical definition. At the impersonal level, the super-ego represents that collection of mores, expectations and rules of behavior that govern "civilized" society. It is the primary agent for the maintenance of civil society and the protection of that society from external forces that would threaten its cohesiveness and from internal forces of chaos. In Western society, the super-ego supports and enforces the mechanisms of civilization. In other societies, the super-ego would be identified with tribal cohesiveness or other cultural forms. At a more basic level, the super-ego can be identified with maintenance of the consensual reality.

At the personal level, the super-ego is a functional element within the psyche of the individual. It tells the ego what it "should" do. (In Freudian psychological terms, it may be said to mediate how the ego "should" interact with the id.) It is the ego's guide to what is expected of it if it is to conform to the societal construct into which it is born. It may be identified as conscience. It is more likely to be an authoritarian voice within the psyche that lays down what rules are to be followed and what actions (and in some cases what thoughts and feelings) are proscribed.

Thus, while the impersonal super-ego is closely identified with the Collective Unconscious, the shape and quality of the personal super-ego, being internal to the psyche, will vary with each individual. Three primary factors come into play in determining the characteristics of the personal super-ego. One is parental influence. Parents, especially the father, are the primary vehicles through which the dictates of the impersonal super-ego are filtered and passed on to the child's psyche. A second factor is the individual's position within society. The super-ego of a business executive differs from that of a ditch digger. These differences are determined, in part, by into what station of society the individual is born and, in part, by the individual's subsequent experience in society. Finally, there is the individual's innate attunement, which may include his/her past life experiences. This factor would explain why a child born into a poor, broken home may be driven by his/her super-ego to succeed in the eyes of society.

The astrological placement of the Midheaven symbolizes the character and qualities of the personal super-ego. They suggest how we may relate to the impersonal super-ego and how our personal super-ego may be transformed. They also suggest how negative behavior—which includes criminality and anti-social behavior--may be manifested when the ego/super-ego relationship is dysfunctional.

Because the super-ego is an important part of the conditioning apparatus of the psyche, its transcendence plays a role in the individuation process symbolized by Uranus. This need to overcome the super-ego as part of individuation is symbolized by the Midheaven's identification with Saturn, and consequent antipathy to Uranus. This process cannot be accomplished, however, simply by resisting or ignoring the super-ego. Instead, the super-ego itself must be transformed so that it points to a spiritual goal.

The Elements and Modalities

Much has been written about the elements and the modalities by Stephen Aroyo and many others. The purpose of this discussion is only to relate these concepts to the Zodiacal signs, to which they primarily associated. There are four elements: fire, earth, air and water. The modalities, which correspond to the Vedic *gunas* are: cardinality, fixity and mutability. The elements and modalities are related to ancient concepts of how the material world is formed and structured. The elements are passive substance and relate to basic qualities of matter. The modalities are active states of motion.

In the Zodiac, the elements and qualities are superimposed on each other through the progression of the signs and the houses. Since the elements are even in number and the modalities are odd in number, each modality successively imbues each element. This produces the magical number twelve. (Note that four and three also produce the liberating number seven and that the relationship between the numbers three and four are symbolized in the pyramid.)

Fire

The fire element is associated with energy and with the activating spirit. Its quality is outgoing, as fire naturally seeks to expand. Fire is associated with the motivating force of life. Its life-spiriting nature generates enthusiasm and a penchant for action. Fire generates warmth, which is comforting and activates the emotions. The fiery emotions tend to be outgoing and to blaze up and die down quickly. These fiery emotions can have intense power for good or destruction. The fire signs are: Aries, Leo, Sagittarius.

Earth

The earth element is associated with solidity and groundedness. Its qualities are stable and enduring. It is the densest element and the most affinity with the physical world. Its density makes it less penetrable than the other elements. The earth element brings cohesiveness and is associated with form and structure (which are the abstract phenomena that hold things together). Density, solidity and structure result in less reactivity, responsiveness and openness than is the case with the other elements. Being the heaviest of the elements, it is the least likely to be moved. It is the strongest of the elements and, thus, capable of supporting weight. It therefore is the symbolic foundation of the created world. Earth is also the element of which building blocks are formed and which are used to erect structures. Thus, the earth element is associated with usefulness and practicality. The earth signs are: Taurus, Virgo, Capricorn.

Air

The air element is associated with the mental realm and with communication. It is the least dense of the elements, as the mental realm contains the least admixture of materiality of the "three realms" (physical, astral and mental). The qualities of the air element are its perviousness, its freedom of movement, its ubiquitousness and its lightness. It is so pervious that light and sound travel through it. Without air, there would be no communication. It touches everything, even being dissolved in water and penetrating the soil. Thus, it is inclined toward social energy and relationships. The air signs are: Gemini, Libra, Aquarius.

Water

The water element is associated with the emotions. Its qualities are fluidity, taking the shape of its container, moistness, lifegivingness, and power. Because it is fluid and malleable, it tends toward changeableness. Its moisture soothes and quenches thirst. Water brings things to life and is sustaining and is therefore associated with caring and nurturing. Yet water, when directed or harnessed, possesses incredible power. Water can also be perfectly still, in which case its tendency is inward. Its tendency to fill empty and, otherwise, hidden cavities symbolizes a need for security, particularly emotional security. The water signs are: Cancer, Scorpio, Pisces.

Cardinality

The cardinal modality symbolizes forward direction and is associated with activity. It is the *rajasik guna* of Vedic cosmology. The cardinal modality is also associated with the initiation of development cycles. It is the thesis of the Hegelian dialectic. Qualities associated with cardinality include confidence, directness of approach and movement toward some goal. The cardinal signs are: Aries, Cancer, Libra, Capricorn.

Fixity

The fixed modality symbolizes inertia and is associated with retentiveness. It is the *tamasik guna* of Vedic cosmology. The fixed modality is associated with the consolidation phase of development cycles. It is the antithesis of the Hegelian dialectic. Qualities associated with fixity include strength, security, immobility and permanence. The fixed signs are: Taurus, Leo, Scorpio, Aquarius.

Mutability

The mutable modality symbolizes balance and duality. Balance (i.e., the equilibrium state between action and inertia) implies duality, since there must be two sides to balance. The mutable modality is the *satvik guna* of the Vedic cosmology. It is associated with the culminating phase of development cycles. It is the synthesis of the Hegelian dialectic. Qualities associated with mutability include pendulum motion, equipoise, instability and uncertainty. The mutable signs are: Gemini, Virgo, Sagittarius, Pisces.

The Houses

Dane Rudhyar and others have written extensively about the houses and their meanings. Traditionally, the houses are seen to represent specific life activities or areas of experience. Rudhyar has conceptualized the house structure as a progression through the developmental phases of life. There are twelve houses, corresponding to the twelve Zodiacal signs and the twelve states derived by combining the sequence of elements and modalities.

First House

The first house symbolizes the self. More specifically, it is associated with the emerging self, the self newly born. It represents the first experiences of the ego in the world and those experiences that continue to relate back to those first experiences. In particular, it is associated with the ego's first awareness of itself and, by extension, the psyche's self-identity. Its first degree is the Ascendant, which symbolizes the persona, a function that is intimately linked to the self-identity. Being the first of the houses, it is seen to represent all types of new beginnings and initiatives. At the transcendent level, the first house symbolizes the discovery of the real self and the actualization of the psyche's true identity.

Second House

The second house symbolizes the psyche's need for basic security. The ego realizes its vulnerability and pulls itself back from its experience of the world. The individual realizes, in the second house, that he/she needs sustenance and the wherewithal with which to survive. For most people, basic security needs are provided through possessions. Having is equated with being secure on the physical level. Thus, the second house has traditionally been seen as the house representing possessions and accumulation.

However, judgment and values also play an important and precursory role in the effort to survive. One must know what is beneficial and harmful and be able to discriminate between the two. It is the psyche's attraction to what will enhance its chances of survival and its repulsion from that which is dangerous and harmful that motivates the ego to try to acquire and experience the "good things in life." Thus, the second house equally represents a person's values and value system. At the transcendent level, the second house symbolizes the transformation of the psyche's value system and the pursuit of those intangibles that will result in real and permanent security.

Third House

Once security in the world is established and the psyche feels safe and well provided for, it can venture once more out into the world. This venturing out is symbolized by the third house. Here, the psyche confronts its immediate environment and begins to explore this. The emphasis in the third house is on direct and immediate experience. Because, developmentally, this phase generally occurs in childhood, the third house has this association with the experiences of childhood. Typically, these include relationships with siblings and childhood friends and these, traditionally, have been associated with the third house. At the transcendent level, the third house symbolizes direct experience of reality unhindered by any preconditioning or ego-interference, through which the consciousness lives only in the Here and Now.

Fourth House

Typically, the psyche discovers that the world outside contains threats and perils, so the next stage of development entails another search for security. This involves a strategic retreat so that the psyche can establish a base in order to secure itself and put itself on a firmer foundation to face the external world. This often involves a return to its roots in order to find that base of security. The association of the fourth house with rootedness is symbolized by its position at the nadir of the horoscope. Typically, the psyche finds the necessary safety and security with close family. Metaphorically, when the young child becomes scared when venturing out into the world, it runs home to find its parents. Thus, the fourth house has traditionally been seen to symbolize family (especially parents), home and, by extension, all things domestic. At the transcendent level, the fourth house symbolizes the True Home of the psyche that it finds when it retreats into itself and seeks its own Origin.

Fifth House

After a sufficient level of security has been established by the psyche, it now feels comfortable in going out into the world again. This time, it does so with a surer sense of itself and a desire to define itself to the world. The fifth house represents the yearning or need to show oneself to the world and gain its acceptance and appreciation. In the fifth house, the psyche tests out the persona that it has fashioned for itself. It is comparable to the psychological developmental stage of "trying on identities." Symbolically, the fifth house is related to the Ascendant (symbolizing the persona) in a trine relationship.

The testing out and display of identity and personality is essentially a self-expressive and creative process. Thus, the fifth house is associated with all types of creativity. This, typically, includes the arts, drama, etc. In our materialistically-oriented world, the fifth house is sometimes associated with creativity in the management of money, e.g. finance. Also, because so many people fail to recognize their own creativity, the fifth house is often primarily associated with that most basic of creative acts—procreation. By extension, the fifth house has come to be associated with children and with that precursor to much initial procreation—romantic love. At the transcendent level, the fifth house is associated with the psyche's ability to merge with and become a tool of the cosmic or divine Creative Force.

Sixth House

Though the fifth house is self-expressive and, therefore, extroverted, it also contains a self-absorptive quality. Once the persona is formed, a process begins whereby the attention of the psyche is turned away from the ego and towards others. The first stage in this process is represented by the sixth house. The sixth house represents the "knocking off of the rough edges" from the persona. Through self-examination and self-refinement, the psyche learns to adapt its persona to take others into consideration.

Self-examination and self-correction is not work that is undertaken readily by most people. Therefore, it is typically undergone unconsciously. The mechanisms that the Collective Unconscious uses to socialize the egotistical persona include work, service and situations that force the ego into a position of humility. Thus, the sixth house is traditionally characterized as the place of work and service. Health matters are also associated with the sixth house. This association takes place because health (or the lack of it) represents the need for self-improvement and correction at the most basic, physical, level. At the transcendent level, the sixth house is symbolizes the examined life and the psyche's yearning to achieve spiritual perfection.

Seventh House

The seventh house represents the completion of the initial phase of self-development—the completion of identity formation and an integral personality—and the beginning of the next phase—the integration of the self with the not-self. That the seventh house represents a radically different phase of self-development is symbolized by the fact that its first degree is the Descendant of the horoscope. The initial step in the integration process of this new development phase is the formation of primary relationship—one on one. Thus, the seventh house symbolizes all forms of inter-personal relationship, but especially marriage (or marriage-like arrangements). Additionally, the seventh house may symbolize partnerships, contracts and other forms of formal relationship. At the transcendent level, the seventh house symbolizes the relationship between the self and the Divine, when the two are considered to be separate entities. The metaphor for this relationship is often given as the relationship between the true lover and the Divine Beloved.

Eighth House

The eighth house symbolizes a maturing of the interpersonal relationship phase of self-development to include intimacy. A basic expression of intimacy is sex and the eighth house is, therefore, associated with sexuality. Intimacy in a relationship typically goes beyond the sharing of physical energy to the sharing of all types of resources—emotional and material. Thus, the eighth house has traditionally represented shared resources. A specific type of sharing of resources occurs after the death of one of the participants in a relationship—bequest. The eighth house ruler—Pluto—is associated with death and this association carries over to the eighth house. Traditionally, the eighth house symbolizes wills and inheritances. At the transcendent level, the eighth house symbolizes spiritual intimacy with the Beloved and the bequest of Love that the Beloved confers on the lover when the lover dies to him/herself.

Ninth House

The ninth house represents a reemergence of the self from the introverted state of intimacy into the wider world again. This time, however, the self seeks to establish its place in a world that is larger than itself. The quest to go beyond the personal self is the defining quality of the ninth house. An important part of this quest is to understand the wider world and the individual's place in it. Thus, the ninth house is traditionally associated with understanding and with those institutions that bring understanding—particularly institutions of higher education. Travel is another way in which the individual broadens his/her horizons and the ninth house has been traditionally associated with this activity. At the transcendent level, the ninth house represents the true understanding of Reality that the self acquires after the experience of spiritual intimacy.

Tenth House

The tenth house represents the establishment of the self in society and the contribution that the individual now makes to society. This is not an altruistic contribution, but the contribution that the individual makes in Adam Smith fashion, while pursuing his/her own self-interest. Nevertheless, there is a sense of responsibility that is associated with tenth house activity. The fact that the first degree of the tenth house is the Midheaven, with its association with the super-ego, symbolizes this sense of responsibility to society. Thus, the tenth house represents all forms of publicly-recognized accomplishment. In particular, the tenth house has traditionally been associated with career and with public life. At the transcendent level, the tenth house represents devotion to a spiritual goal and the discipline required to achieve spiritual heights.

Eleventh House

The eleventh house symbolizes that stage of development in which the individual realizes that there is something lacking in his/her quest for public recognition and accomplishment and decides to give back to society altruistically. Thus, the eleventh house represents social responsibility. It is associated with humanitarian efforts and causes for the betterment of humanity. The eleventh house also represents that stage where the psyche undertakes its individuation away from the conditioning of the Collective Unconscious. For most people, this process of differentiation is accomplished only partially and results in group-identity. Thus, the eleventh house has traditionally been associated with groups and clubs, as well as the social friendship that these institutions provide. At the transcendent level, the eleventh house represents true and complete individuation and the recognition by the self of its true nature—i.e., Self-realization.

Twelfth House

The twelfth house is, admittedly, the most complicated of the houses, for it represents the end of the cycle of development and the seeds for the beginning of a new development cycle. It is the reaping ground of life's journey. Whatever progress, or lack of progress, the individual has made in his/her self-development is reflected in the experiences symbolized by the twelfth house.

It is difficult to talk about the twelfth house without involving the theories of karma and reincarnation. For, the reward (or punishment) for past endeavors does not only occur at the end the physical life, in old age (with which the twelfth house is associated). Twelfth house experiences are occurring throughout life and the house has a strong association with karmic payback. For too many people, this karmic payback brings pain and suffering and the twelfth house has traditionally been associated with this aspect. Furthermore, pain and suffering is most likely to occur at the end of life. It may be seen as a type of cleansing in preparation for the next life (developmental cycle).

Typically, near the end of life, people will experience a greater degree of confinement than they had previously in life, whether this confinement be the inability to get around as much as before or confinement in a nursing home or—particularly at the final stage—in a hospital or hospice. The twelfth house has come to symbolize all of these institutions of confinement and preparation for death. Confinement may also be punitive and, so, the twelfth house has come to symbolize prisons and all other types of imprisonment. The prison symbolism also relates to karmic punishment. Prison also involves the entire judicial and correctional system. The twelfth house also symbolizes the Day of Judgment experienced after death (and, if one believes, where one's future karmic destiny is determined).

None of these are pleasant associations for most people and, therefore, the twelfth house has been traditionally categorized as malefic. Karmic events seem to come upon people from out of nowhere. People disappear out of sight when they are confined. Thus, the twelfth house has also been associated with "things hidden." To the spiritually aware, however, the hidden world is more real than the consensual reality. In pursuit of the hidden treasure of spirituality, the individual willingly undergoes isolation, asceticism and self-denial. He/she pays strict attention to the karmic consequences of his/her action.

At its transcendent level, the twelfth house leads to spiritual liberation. It leads to a new cycle of development on a higher plane of consciousness. Ultimately, it leads to the total merging of the self with the Infinite.

The Signs

As mentioned previously, the Zodiacal signs symbolize qualities with which the planetary functions are invested. The function works through these qualities, as through a medium. The particular medium symbolized by the Zodiacal sign colors the operations of the planetary function, so that these functions seem to act according to those qualities and characteristics associated with the sign.

The sign itself carries an essential meaning that is then manifested in diverse ways at many levels of consciousness. The essential meaning of the sign is, itself, derived from a composite of symbolic influences, beginning with the ruling planet and including its associated element, modality, house and representative glyph. Much, indeed, has been written about the meanings of signs and, so, what follows is simply a summary distillation.

Aries

The essential quality of Aries is that of initial forward motion. This is seen in the symbol for Mars, its ruling planet, which features a vector indicating directed motion (action). This is also symbolized by it being the first sign of the Zodiac, associated with the first house, and by its glyph, which can be seen as representing the sprouting of a seed as it first breaks ground. With respect to consciousness, Aries is associated with the psyche's initial self-awareness. This, it derives from its association with the developmental role of the first house.

Action and activity are strong qualities of Aries. Aries is ruled by Mars, the planet symbolizing the function of taking action. It is the cardinal fire sign and both cardinality and fire symbolize active principles—cardinality, the quality of forward moving action and fire, the quality of energetic action. Thus, Aries is very strongly associated with the quality of active energy. The particular quality of this active energy is that it is that which initially occurs. Thus, Aries is associated with all types of qualities relating to this energy, such as impulsiveness, assertiveness, eagerness (especially eagerness to begin), enthusiasm for new endeavor, etc.

Aries' glyph is more traditionally seen to represent the ram (the horns of the ram, specifically). This, again, is symbolic of impulsiveness (the ram's propensity to charge) and forward (charging) motion. The (male) ram's aggressive tendencies, too, relate to the Aries qualities. The strong horns of the ram protruding from its head symbolize the headstrong tendencies associated with Aries. Mars, the god of war, also contributes to the association of aggression and martial qualities with Aries.

The fire element contributes to Aries' impulsive tendencies, as flames are apt to suddenly reach out. Fire is not inhibited by any internal restraints. It produces heat (fiery emotion) and light (objectivity). The objectivity associated with Aries is also a property related to Mars, for action, to be effective, must be practical and applied according to the rules of the objective universe. The emotional component of the Aries quality is related most to desire (symbolized by Mars). Ardent desire can be said to be typically Aries.

Taking action and moving forward (Mars and cardinal qualities) are intrinsically linked to initiation (of action and direction) and newness (which is what is always encountered when one moves forward). Beginnings, inexperience, self-consciousness and innocence or naiveté are all Aries qualities that can be associated with the firstness of Aires, as well as the meanings of its glyph—both the sprout and the newly born spring ram.

The concept of self, derived from Aries association with the first house and its developmental function of the emerging self-identity, is an important component of the Aries quality. Aries has a quality of being self-referenced. Thus, Aries' active energy proceeds from the desire of the self. The self-referencing of this active energy produces self-assertiveness, self-will, self-consciousness and naïve selfishness.

The more the Aries energy operates from the ego, the harsher and negative the Aries qualities tend to be. The obsession with the ego-self and its need for affirmation typically results in such Aries qualities as pushiness, thoughtless insensitivity to the needs of others, aggression and self-centeredness. The maturing of the self-identity and the development of selflessness produces those noble qualities associated with Aries, such as courage, leadership, straightforwardness and decisiveness in action. At the transcendent level, Aries symbolizes the finding of the True Self, a return to Innocence and right-action taken with no thought of reward.

Taurus

The essential quality of Taurus is enduringness, in its passive state, and organicness in its active mode. Organicness is actually the active manifestation of enduringness, for it is through organic cycles of generation and growth that enduringness is preserved. These organic cycles reach their full expression in the Scorpio energy, which encompasses not only birth and growth, but also death and rebirth.

Taurus is ruled by the planet Venus and it is the evaluative function symbolized by Venus that finds prominence in Taurus. Awareness of what is good, pleasant and preserving as opposed to what is harmful, unpleasant and destructive is essential if the psyche is to be able to physically survive and endure. The element of physical survival and well-being is symbolized by Venus' glyph of the circle (consciousness) placed over the cross of materiality, signifying the rulership of consciousness over materiality through discriminating evaluation and the dependency of consciousness on the body for its existence (on the physical plane, at least).

The association of Taurus with the material is given additional weight by its being an earth sign. That which is physical, manifested and substantial is important in the Taurean view and Taurean qualities are clothed in association with the physical. The guiding principle represented by Venus when applied to the materially substantive earth element necessarily brings forth practicality and a conservatively pragmatic approach in the Taurean character—qualities that result in preservation and enduringness.

Earth when combined with Venusian fecundity brings forth fruitfulness and organic abundance. Thus, Taurus is associated with the slow and steady processes of organic growth. Taurus is the fixed earth sign and this fixity, in the context of organic earth, becomes rootedness and an association with plantlike qualities, especially with the longevity of trees and other firmly rooted plants. It is a Taurean characteristic to thrive in home soil, which is tried and true and sustaining, and to resist uprooting.

At its extreme, this fixed earthiness becomes rock hard and immovable. This symbolizes not only strength and the ability to support great structures built on its foundation, but also stubbornness and rigidity. If the organic life force departs through petrification, there is a danger that the warm emotions symbolized by the warm and fertile soil become turned to stone, manifesting only as resistance.

The fixed modality is often associated with a need for security and in combination with the earth element this expresses itself as a need for physical security. Enduringness is, therefore, most often expressed as a will to physically endure. When the Taurean sense of physical security is threatened, the natural reaction is often to buttress the physical well-being of the Taurean through acquisition of more of the means of sustenance. This drive to acquire may become compulsive or domineering if the Taurus-dominated psyche is particularly insecure.

The urge to survive and endure that is central to the Taurean character is enabled by the ability to acquire and possess the means of survival. Taurus' association with the second house brings to it a strong association with possessiveness, the desire for physical security and comfort, and enjoyment of material abundance and sensual gratification. These characteristics are strengthened through the rulership of Venus (which informs both Taurus and the second house) and its function of attracting what is pleasant and beneficial.

Taurus' glyph, the bull, embodies all of these qualities and adds its own symbolism to the mix. Slow moving and patient, it endures all circumstances. It fertilizes the earth, from which it gains its own sustenance, completing the organic cycle of survival. It can stubbornly dig in its heels and become immovable. Set in motion, the bull is an irresistible object. Seemingly docile, when threatened or enraged it becomes dangerous in its sudden violence. The bull is basically instinctual and in its quest for survival of its species becomes a symbol of animal passion. When harnesses and domesticated, the bull will pull the heaviest loads, plod along steadily over the same ground repeatedly and bear intolerable burdens. All of these qualities are associated with the Taurus energy.

When it is the ego that is striving to endure and survive, the Taurean qualities are manifested as possessiveness and extreme attachment to material existence. The Taurean holds close that which will ensure his/her comfortable survival. The animal nature symbolized by the bull holds full reign over the psyche. The appetites of the instinctual nature are unchecked. Indulgence in sensual gratification, violent rages, unreasonable stubbornness are all symptoms of this state. Alternatively, the psyche may become so obsessed with the goal of physical preservation that the single-minded Taurean pursuit of sustenance results in a brute, dull existence, dominated by drudgery and routine.

The Taurus glyph can also be interpreted abstractly, however, providing clues as to the transcendent meaning of the sign. The closed circle represents the world, or the consciousness inhabiting the physical world, while the half circle above it is open to the heavens. Thus, the transcendent Taurean energy is "in the world, but not of it." The spiritual side of the psyche (the container open to higher levels of consciousness emanating from "above") is supported by material existence (the circle of organic life). Thus, the realized Taurean does his/her duty in the material world, "giving to Caesar that which is Caesar's," but turns his/her heart upward and inward. The bull now becomes a symbol, not of animal passion, but rather or devotion which sublimates and overcomes animal passion, the lower tendencies of the psyche. Freed of these attachments to the concerns of a material existence, the Taurean consciousness discriminatingly contemplates the perfect balance (Venus) in which everything is seen to be good and in its rightful state.

Gemini

The essential quality of Gemini is multi-facetedness. Multi-facetedness occasions several related qualities that are necessary in order for multi-facetedness to manifest. These qualities include freedom from being tied down to any one thing or viewpoint, lightness accompanied by detachment, and facility and speed. The latter allow the consciousness to move quickly from one thing to another, giving the impression of being able to handle several things at once.

Gemini is ruled by Mercury. Thus, mental energy tends to be the predominant quality of Gemini. This does not necessarily imply an intellectual approach. Often, it is communication or know-how that are paramount expressions of the mental energy characterizing Gemini. Mercury, the winged messenger of the Romans, epitomizes the qualities of swiftness and talkativeness that are associated with Gemini.

Gemini is the mutable air sign. The air element, which is associated with the mental plane, contributes along with Mercury to the mental orientation that is typical of Gemini. Gemini generally possesses the quality of experiencing the world through knowing it. The air element also symbolizes the openness and freedom that the Gemini energy gravitates toward. Clarity and lightness are other qualities that the element bestows on Gemini.

The mutable mode contributes to the changeableness and constant activity that is associated with Gemini. Typically, the Gemini activity is not sustained and directed, but rather going in one direction and then another. The butterfly, a denizen of the air whose wings move rapidly from one side of its pendulum motion to the other, is often identified with Gemini. Like the butterfly that flits from here to there, never resting for more than a few seconds, Gemini can rarely stand to be still or, at the psychological level, to be committed to the point of feeling hemmed in and trapped.

Gemini is associated with the third house, which represents immediate experience. Thus, the Gemini energy is typically associated with a desire for the immediate and an inability to direct attention to that which is remote in time or space. Gemini energy is generally directed at experiencing everything around us, all at once (like the air which is all around). Once experienced, or as experienced, Gemini usually translates this experience into mental form and then communicates it.

The immediacy that Gemini desires also extends to the dimension of depth. Depth generally takes time, commitment and concentration of attention—all traits that are not those attributable to Gemini. Instead, the Gemini energy is attracted to the surface, where little resistance to movement is met and from which Gemini's Mercurial attention can easily pick up and go.

Gemini's glyph—the Twins—has often been interpreted as representing an essential duality, seconded by Gemini's mutability. Duality implies that there are opposites. While the Gemini energy may be more prone than most signs to such dualities as being up and down or back and forth, duality is not a predominant quality of Gemini. Twins are not normally opposite mirrors of each other, though they are often different from each other.

Rather than duality, the primary meaning of the Twins glyph is Gemini's capacity to handle simultaneous difference and its quest for multiple experiences. Two can simply experience twice as much as can one and it is this desire for maximum experience and for not being tied to a single point of view that is represented by Gemini's twinness. Being able to put on two faces at once means that one does not have to be committed to either. Seeing both sides—or rather all sides—means that the psyche can engage in multiple experience. It is not irresoluteness, necessarily, that the Gemini energy displays, but the capacity to support both sides at once. Thus, Gemini is the perfect modality with which to existentially experience the world. In the end, knowing that the other side is just as valid as one's own point of view, the Gemini personality can conclude that "it doesn't matter."

When the psyche is consumed in its own point of view, this existential outlook easily becomes callous indifference. The Geminian desire for freedom to experience when not tempered with compassion results in a cruel lack of commitment to others' feelings. In this state, the Geminian thinks only of his/her own pleasure. He/she chooses not to look beyond the surface of his/her own ego perception and is, therefore, wantonly unaware of the harm that he/she may be causing others.

At the transcendent level, however, freedom and detachment are expressed in terms of the mind's freedom from material bondage. Lack of commitment to any one material entity or subjective point of view, when mixed with compassion, becomes commitment to everything and the validation of all points of view. The Gemini energy is raised to the level where all exists in the Here and Now and experience is totally immediate through direct perception of Reality.

Cancer

The essential quality of Cancer is emotional response. Emotional response carries as its precondition the state of feeling, which is also closely associated with Cancer. Feeling and emotional response become diversified and particularized as they are in touch with various media and situations. Thus, when the psyche feels threatened, the emotional response is to protect; when the psyche feels pity, the emotional response is to give sympathy; when the psyche feels needed, the emotional response is to nurture; and when the psyche feels injured, the emotional response will be negative.

Cancer is ruled by the Moon, which is associated both with basic emotions and with responsiveness. The Moon also symbolizes motherhood and family in general. This relates to Cancer's nurturing characteristics and also symbolizes the protective role associated with Cancer. Family relates to domesticity, which is also symbolized by the fourth house, with which Cancer is linked. Thus, Cancer has been traditionally associated with domestic tendencies, a caring attitude and mothering qualities.

Cancer is the cardinal water sign. The water element intensifies Cancer's association with emotion, giving Cancer the reputation as the most emotional of the signs. The cardinal modality provides action and force behind Cancer's emotionality. Cancer typically expresses its emotionality, even if this expression is passive. The Cancerian emotion is directed. Even when the Cancerian psyche appears to be overwhelmed by emotion, it is usually aimed at someone or something and is usually being expressed for some purpose or is motivating the individual toward some end.

The fact that Cancer is not often seen as possessing a steadfast quality is due to the influences of water and the Moon overpowering the quality of cardinality. The Moon, with its phases and its influence on the tides, possesses an alternating rhythm that, when applied to the emotions, results in moodiness or changeable emotions. Cancerian emotions are basically reactive and, therefore, change depending on with what the feeling-response mechanism has come in contact.

·The fourth house, besides symbolizing domesticity in Cancer, also brings its association with rootedness. In some, this may be manifested as homeboundness, while in others it is expressed as an attunement and attraction to the subconscious. The Moon, too, has a strong association with the subconscious. Thus, intuition is a Cancerian quality, especially gut-intuition that comes from deep within an emotional state of mind.

Cancer's glyph is the crab. At first glance, the crab does not seem to be an embodiment of emotionality. The crab, however, represents the other side of Cancer, strongly associated with the withdrawing tendencies of the fourth house. It has often been said that Cancer's feeling mechanism is so sensitive to outside environmental influences that it must be protected. This is symbolized by the very reactive and sensitive body of the crab that is surrounded by a hard, defensive shell.

Thus, to protect him/herself, the Cancerian personality often surrounds him/herself with defense mechanisms, most likely those of withdrawal, seeming indifference, reservation and masking of the real personality. Like the crab, when the Cancerian psyche feels threatened, it may lash out in response with the intent of causing pain to the threatening party. When the Cancerian emotional psyche has been hurt to severely or too many times, the retreat into its shell may become permanent and it may take great effort for the psyche to emotionally open up again.

An alternative interpretation of the Cancerian glyph is a representation of the female breasts. These symbolize the life-giving, nurturing aspect of the Cancer energy. At the transcendent level, they symbolize the Earth Mother and the womb of the subconscious, into which the psyche returns in order to return to a state of innocence. This return, however, takes place after experience and so, rather than returning to a state of naïve innocence, the psyche consciously realizes that the nurturing and security that it seeks can only be found by returning to its Source. The return Home is accompanied by the development of great powers of intuition and compassion and an extraordinary capacity to give of oneself.

Leo

The essential quality of Leo is self-expressiveness. This often occurs in a dramatic fashion, because to express oneself one must be noticed. Typically, a quality of Leo is a deep need to be recognized and appreciated. This need drives us to craft a persona that will be taken seriously by the rest of the world.

Leo is ruled by the Sun. The Sun not only symbolizes the self, but also the expression of the self as represented by the rays of the Sun. Without its rays to carry its light, the Sun would be invisible. When it shines, the Sun is evident to all (for even the blind can feel its warmth). The Leo quality emulates the Sun in wanting to shine and be seen by others. The shining quality of Leo also suggests that to attract attention to the self, certain positive qualities are to be cultivated. For, no one would want to attract attention to what is dark and ugly, unless that person had such a perverse need for attention that he/she is willing to obtain it in any way possible.

Leo is the fixed fire sign, like the Sun that, from the terra-centric viewpoint, is a ball of stationary fire. The fire element suggests a will to act. In its fixed state, however, it is not likely that this is a will to be in action, but rather a will to cause action. From this, Leo gains an association with command, by which a king, while himself unmoving, causes his will to be carried out. What more effective way to be noticed than to have the ability to command?

The fire element is also associated with the warm emotions. The fixing of these emotions makes them strong and powerful. This produces an intense warmth of emotion. Again, however, the desire is to attract attention and positive recognition, so the typical Leo desire is for others to come to him/her in order to receive the warmth of his/her fire, the largesse of the king. Like the generous king, it is a Leonine quality to give freely, but it is also typical of Leo to expect gratitude, appreciation and loyalty in return.

The fixed modality is often associated with a need for security and in combination with the fire element this is expressed as a need for security of identity (securing the inner fire or light of beingness). The threat to identity (the existential threat that your light may be extinguished) is generally countered by the forceful expression of your identity to the world. By seeing your identity, in the form of a persona, being active in the world, your sense of identity is reaffirmed. The more threatened the Leo identity feels, the more compulsively and domineeringly the persona is likely to be expressed.

Leo is associated with the fifth house, which is the house of creativity and the expression of the persona. The latter directly relates to the Leonine essence. It is often characteristic of Leo to express creativity or to be attracted to creative pursuits. This is especially true if there is an element of showmanship or drama involved. The fixed nature of Leo often prevents an expression of childlikeness that could be connected with the fifth house's association with children, but the immature Leo often expresses qualities of childishness.

Leo's glyph is the lion's mane and qualities associated with the king of beasts permeate Leo. The Leonine desire for authority and respect has already been mentioned. Pride is naturally associated with the desire to express oneself and be noticed, for it is normal to take pride in what you have created. Loyalty is another quality associated with the lion and this is a quality that the Leo personality both possesses and expects from others. Like the lion, when injured or cornered it is characteristic of Leo to turn ferocious and dangerous.

When possessed by the lower self, the tendency of the Leo energy is to be about domination, self-importance, egotistic pride and showing off. The psyche is easily overcome by anger and passion. Injuries to pride are not easily forgotten and the Leo will stalk his/her prey until the time is right to pounce and return the injury. The Leo self-pride will seldom allow the individual to admit that he/she is wrong. On the other hand, the insecure Leo personality is constantly craving validation and attention and may be willing to debase him/herself in order to gain attention. Or, filled with stage-fright, the Leo personality may be more like that of the cowardly lion.

At the transcendent level, the Leo character rises to nobility. The kingly/queenly attributes of generosity, compassionate benevolence, mercy and true leadership come to the fore. The self is ever cognizant that its light does not originate from its own selfhood, but from a deeper and more powerful source. The realized person sees that he/she is not the doer, but that there is another Doer acting through him/her. He/she, therefore, participates in the creation being at one with the Creative Force and realizing his/her true servanthood to the One.

Virgo

The essential quality of Virgo is perfection. The drive for perfection is manifested in a variety of ways as the Virgoan energy takes concrete form. Thus, Virgo symbolizes perfection at all levels, from the physical to the spiritual. It also is associated with the means by which perfection may be achieved.

Virgo is ruled by Mercury, which symbolizes the mental, communicative and nervous functions. The mental qualities are, therefore, predominant in Virgo. It is the mind, more than anything else, that is used to guide those functions and areas of life associated with Virgo toward perfection. To achieve perfection, the mind must have a clear idea of the current state of affairs and how this state of affairs is imperfect. Only by recognizing the imperfect can the corrective measures that will lead to perfection be taken. Therefore, it is common for Virgo to be associated with attention to the negative, through criticism, dissatisfaction, close examination and exactitude.

Virgo is the mutable earth sign. The mental energy symbolized by the Mercury rulership interacts with the earth element and Virgo's mutability to produce qualities that blend these three energies together. The combination of earth and the airiness inherent in Mercury manifests as a dominating motif of the process of concretization, or the bringing down of the abstract to practical levels. Thus, it is a Virgoan quality to deal with the abstract and the practical, simultaneously, and to apply the abstract to the practical. Analysis is a primary mode of using the abstract to attain practical ends. Analysis can also be seen as a process that takes the purely abstract and makes it accessible and utilitarian. The mutable mode also plays into the realization of Virgo's analytical quality, in that the application of mutability to earth results in a constant sifting of mental construct and shifting from levels of the abstract to those of greater and greater concreteness.

The combination of mutability and earth also leads to a process of particularization. The constant back and forth movement of earth breaks down its solidity into finer and finer particles. This, again, is symbolic of the Virgoan tendency to move from the abstract and universal to the concrete and specific. It manifests in the Virgoan attraction to detail and interest in the minutely defined.

Virgo is associated with the sixth house, which is the house that represents self-refinement, self-improvement and, traditionally, work and health. Thus, the Virgo energy is generally concerned with these matters. It is not uncommon for the Virgoan drive for perfection to be expressed as a concern for perfect health or, its negative aspect, hypochondria. The Virgoan association with work and service is generally expressed in qualities such as diligence and conscientiousness. It is also a typical Virgoan quality to be focused on improving the self and aiming for a state of perfection. Thus, perfectionism and self-criticism are typical Virgo traits.

Virgo's glyph represents the virgin, who symbolizes the state of purity and perfection. This is not a state of innocence, because at the stage of development symbolized by the sixth house, much has been experienced. Rather, this is an attempt to return to purity out of the messiness of experience. This fact colors the Virgoan nature considerably.

As stated above, the quality of purity manifests itself at all levels in the Virgo nature. At the physical level, it is expressed as a desire for cleanliness, neatness and everything being in its proper place. The latter is also a result of Virgo's proclivity to analyze, which entails categorization. The emotions are often perceived, from the Virgoan perspective, as messy, problematic and even impure. Therefore, there is a tendency in Virgo to disengage from the emotional sphere and to protect ourselves against disruptive emotions. The emotional experience is often replaced by an adherence to objectivism and an attraction toward the pragmatic.

Morality is often used as a devise to cleanse the psyche of impurities. Morality, in the Virgoan context, includes not only truthfulness and ethical behavior, but properness and conformity to social mores. The typical Virgo behavior is to always color within the lines and use the correct colors, metaphorically applied to all aspects of life. Because of the strong compulsion that the Virgo-dominated psyche feels to abide by conventional morality, the Virgoan outlook is sometimes judgmental and puritanical, with the Virgo native applying his/her own standards to the behavior of others.

When the psyche is ego-centered, the Virgo energy can express itself in a number of ways. One of these is to become so obsessively focused on ourselves that the result is a blaming, overly critical attitude that is directed both at ourselves and others. The reason for blame is, of course, that nothing is perfect in this imperfect world. Frustrated by the failure to realize the Virgoan expectation of purity and perfection, the afflicted Virgo energy often expresses itself in the opposite direction from the traditional Virgoan fastidiousness. The afflicted Virgoan energy results in disorganization, becoming flustered over details, messiness and lack of personal hygiene, often accompanied by guilt. This state is usually the result of us taking the entire burden of perfection upon ourselves.

At the transcendent level, Virgo becomes concerned with spiritual purity and the attainment of the perfection of the soul. This begins with sincere repentance, the cleansing of the psyche of bad habits and immoral behavior and surrender to a spiritual discipline. Humility is a necessary ingredient that must be added to the aspirant's state of consciousness. The one embarking on this path of purity then must polish the mirror of the heart until it is completely free of all defects. Then, and only then, may the psyche gaze into this mirror to discover the True Self.

Libra

The essential quality of Libra is harmony achieved through balance and equipoise. This drive to experience harmony and tranquility is manifested both internally and externally. In its external manifestation it, inevitably involves other people and, so, the achievement of social harmony and the conditions necessary for social harmony to occur are closely associated with Libra.

Libra is ruled by Venus. It is the relationship function symbolized by Venus that is predominantly expressed through Libra. Yet, the evaluative function associated with Venus also plays a strong role in forming the Libra character. For, it is typically Libran to be concerned about form and to appreciate beauty. External and internal harmony is achieved, in part, by surrounding yourself with harmonious and beautiful things. There is a strong element in Libra of attraction to the beautiful and repulsion by the ugly—in other words, of constant judgment upon the state of affairs in which the Libran finds him/herself.

Libra is the cardinal air sign. One might expect the qualities of harmony and equipoise to be a product of the mutable modality, but mutability would paralyze the already indecisive Libra energy and allow it to be entirely too passive. Instead, the cardinal modality pushes the Libran energy forward to actualize itself in the world through engagement in interpersonal relationship and the creation and maintenance of harmony. Air is the natural element for the social expression that is inherently Libran. The mental energy associated with air is also evident in the Libran character, as the Libran is mentally aware of his/her world and thinks about harmony and social interaction, although the feeling element, represented by Venus' rulership, is not absent.

Libra is associated with the seventh house and, therefore, with the dichotomy of self and other. Although all houses are, of course, in opposition, it is the first-seventh house opposition that is the defining archetype and it is the seventh house that brings the opposition into being. Libra, therefore, more than any other sign, is vulnerable to the qualities associated with opposition. Thus, the self-other conflict is generally a part of the Libran experience. Libra is notoriously vulnerable to being influenced by others, both externally and internally. It is common for the Libra-dominated psyche to place primary consideration on how his/her own actions will affect others and, thus, his/her relationships with others.

The seventh house, being the house of relationships, when combined with the Venus and air associations, makes Libra especially conscious of the relationship aspect of everything Relationship is a primary sphere within the Libra energy attempts to create and preserve harmony. The disruption of harmony within the social context is, perhaps, the worst that can be experienced in from the Libran viewpoint. The Libra-dominated native is, therefore, often willing to sacrifice anything, not the least his/her own will, convenience and even identity, to preserve social harmony. This sometimes results in the apparent disappearance of the self altogether or the substitution of the self with a superficial persona that is fashioned only to get others to like us.

The glyph that represents Libra is the scale or balance. The balance symbolizes the states of equipoise and harmony, for harmony implies that there is no dissonant imbalance between two (or more) entities. Balance is also what is needed in the face of Libran dichotomy between self and other. The scale is the instrument of weighing and, therefore, of taking stock and evaluating, It is, thus, consistent with the evaluative function symbolized by Libra's ruling planet, Venus. It represents the mental state of Libra, which is constant evaluation and taking stock in order to perceive the potential imbalances within a situation and act to correct them. The scales also symbolize justice and suggest the keen awareness of justice and injustice which can be a Libran quality.

When the Libran psyche is ego-dominated, all of the thoughts and actions undertaken by us are to gain affection from others and protect the ego from rejection. You may think that your concern is only for others, but in reality it is for what others will think of you and how they will treat you. The irony of this position is that the authentic self is sacrificed for a superficial self that is dominated by the expectations of others so that the ego can feel safe and "in harmony" with your social environment. Yet, the ego remains extremely vulnerable. It takes everything personally so that, if it is not the center of social attention, it feels neglected and insecure. Generally, the insecure individual will try to turn attention back to ourselves by engaging others.

At the transcendent level, the Libran energy seeks a true harmony. Apparent harmony can be disrupted and the insecure Libran psyche cannot abide the appearance of disharmony in his/her environment. Transcending this ego-based perception, the individual realizes the essential harmony that exists when the oneness of all Creation is realized. He/she tries to realize this harmony within him/herself by cultivating a state of psychic and spiritual equipoise. When all of the forces of the psyche are brought into balance and everything is seen to fit together with perfection, the self is united with the Self and the Grand Harmony, the music of the spheres, is heard.

Scorpio

The essential quality of Scorpio is that of intensity and, particularly, emotional intensity. It is Scorpio's nature to raise everything to a more concentrated level of experience. There is a capacity to feel everything as more real and alive and there is a capacity to feel everything as immediately personal. Yet, for Scorpio, the personal is always in relation to others. The Scorpionic intensity is expressed in various forms. At the physical level, it manifests in the intense emotional intimacy of sexuality. Within the social context, it often takes shape in terms of concern about power relationships. The most intense emotions are associated with Scorpio. At the mental-psychic level, Scorpionic intensity is expressed as insight and intuition.

Pluto is Scorpio's ruling planet. Pluto is associated with the intensity of transformation through crisis and both crisis and transformation can be expressed in the Scorpio energy. A common Scorpio quality is to generally treat those circumstances that are met with in life from a crisis viewpoint. Every decision becomes a critical decision upon which personal success and failure depend. At this heightened level of criticality, it is natural that the Scorpio consciousness takes the psychic time to calculate his/her actions in order to manipulate his/her circumstances (including other people) to his/her advantage. When this course is taken, interpersonal relations become relations of power—power and will being functions that are symbolized by Pluto.

Not only power and sexuality, but the full range of psychological function symbolized by Pluto can be clearly expressed through Scorpio. One such function is the stripping away of falsehood to reveal uncompromising truth. This strong attraction to, even obsession with, truth has sometimes lead to others seeing the Scorpio-persona as insensitive to the feelings of others, blunt and overly harsh in his/her judgments. On the other hand, if negativity dominates the Scorpio consciousness, "truth" may be victimized and manipulated to serve the ends of the ego.

Scorpio is the fixed water sign. The water element brings an emotional quality to Scorpio well beyond the emotional implications derived from Pluto. The fixed modality emphasizes the intensity that emotion is subjected to in Scorpio. As in a deep pool of still water, the Scorpionic emotions are drawn up from the deep places of the psyche and the subconscious. Having such core associations, they tend to be powerful in nature. The fixed modality suggests the possibility of intense pressure, which calls forth the metaphor of pressurized steam, another power-laden force. Scorpio's intense emotions are frequently behind an unbendable will. When positively channeled, Scorpio's intense emotions manifest as self-sacrificing loyalty, firm determination, well-directed passion and intense spiritual yearning. When negatively manifested, such traditionally Scorpionic emotions as hatred, revenge, jealousy, spite and lust for power and/or sexuality are the result.

The fixed modality also is associated with a need for security and in combination with the water element this is expressed as a need for emotional security. Despite the intensity of emotion of which it is capable and the capacity to express these emotions forcefully, the Scorpio psyche feels emotionally vulnerable. There is a natural tendency to protect the psyche from threats to its emotional well-being. These threats inevitably derive from the outside—from others who would, intentionally or unintentionally, do you emotional harm. This sense of emotional vulnerability can produce suspicion and even paranoia on the part of the Scorpio-dominated psyche. The defense mechanism often adopted when the world is perceived as threatening and hostile is to strike first, overpower potential enemies and gain the upper hand. These defensive mechanisms have contributed to the traditional association of Scorpio with ruthlessness, cruelty and vindictiveness.

Another way in which to satisfy Scorpio's need for emotional security is through possessive emotional intimacy. The eighth house, which is associated with Scorpio, is the house that represents intimacy and all of the most intimate aspects of life and human relationship. The Scorpio-dominated psyche often has a strong need for intimacy, including sexuality, privacy and secrecy. Despite the introverted nature of intimacy, Scorpio's overriding intensity usually results in the expression or projection of these qualities through the psyche or persona. Intensity, when combined with interpersonal intimacy, also frequently results in a strong psychic bond being formed between the Scorpio native and others. This is generally experienced by others as charisma or a magnetic personality.

The scorpion is generally recognized as Scorpio's glyph. It has been increasingly propounded, however, that the Scorpio glyph undergoes transformation as the level of consciousness attained by the psyche rises and that its glyph becomes metamorphosized into first the eagle and then the phoenix. At the level of the scorpion, the glyph represents all of those qualities traditionally associated with Scorpio as a "malefic" sign—a poisonous nature, ready to strike, watchful and protective of itself, hiding until the right opportunity presents itself and an enemy that one does not want to make. When the consciousness climbs out from dark place under the rock of the ego and ascends into the air as the eagle, it takes on a more authentic power. The keen eye of the eagle represents its insightfulness. Although its swift and certain power may be used to rid the world of mice and vermin, the eagle still acts for its own benefit.

The rulership of Scorpio by one of the outer planets symbolizes the challenge, greater than with most other signs, that its energy brings. The Scorpio energy can easily bring the consciousness to the level of a crawling, vindictive crustacean, associated with evil and death and concerned with the most basic animal drives of sexuality and power. Even when the level of consciousness is raised, it is difficult for the Scorpio energy to overcome its ego-motivated nature and it may continue to "hunt for prey."

Reaching the transcendent level of the Scorpio energy is no easy task, as is symbolized by the Phoenix, who must be consumed in the fire of purification and (the ego) reduced to ashes before rising up transformed. Yet the transformation represented by the Phoenix is not the final stage or even a resting place. For Scorpio is the eighth, not the final sign of the Zodiac. The Phoenix, after laying her egg, dies. And the process of struggle and transformation begins anew. Thus, the Scorpio transformation is a constant and continuous process that continues throughout life. If the struggle is continued, however, the consciousness rises to greater and greater heights.

Sagittarius

The essential quality of Sagittarius is its questing nature. This questingness can manifest unconsciously as restlessness or highly consciously as a directed spiritual focus. In everything that the Sagittarius nature approaches, however, it is never satisfied to be still or look back at the past. Its focus is always on what is over the next horizon. This focus and yearning is evident whether the Sagittarius energy is applied at the physical, emotional, mental or spiritual level.

At the physical level, the Sagittarian energy can be expressed as almost a nervous restlessness, wanderlust, abundant physical energy or directed physical activity (e.g., action sports). At the emotional level, there can be an abundance of lively emotionality, joie de vivre and optimism. Mentally, there is often a yearning to know and to understand, an insatiable curiosity or a tendency to make mental leaps (including jumping to conclusions). Spiritually, the Sagittarian energy becomes an intense spiritual yearning and a hunger for the spiritual quest.

Sagittarius is ruled by Jupiter. The expansiveness that is associated with Jupiter accentuates and powers the Sagittarian questingness. Jupiterian expansiveness pushes the Sagittarian energy outward and "over there." To meet and go beyond the horizon presumes a sense of ability to expand toward that horizon. The good will and beneficence that is associated with Jupiter contributes to the Sagittarian qualities of optimism and good naturedness. The Jupiterian link to established patterns and encompassing social constructs also flavors the Sagittarian energy and makes it susceptible to judgmentalism, for the Jupiterian consciousness "knows" the way things are and should be.

Sagittarius is the mutable fire sign. The fire element infuses Sagittarius with energy and a proclivity toward action. Fire, too, is an expansive element and this combines with Jupiter's rulership to heighten Sagittarius's outgoingness. Fire contributes to the fiery emotionality that Sagittarius can express. The mutable modality only intensifies the fiery energy within Sagittarius. It is like wind whipping ashes into flame or blowing tongues of flame first in one direction, then in another. The tranquility and balance sometimes associated with mutability is very difficult to achieve with the fire element, which is naturally so active, so it is only when the fire energy is sublimated that one can conceive of the Sagittarian in a tranquil state.

Sagittarius is associated with the ninth house, which is the house of understanding and also of sport and travel. The ninth house relates to the Sagittarian capacity to go beyond concern for the ego and to focus on the world around. The ninth house, and its ruler Jupiter, bring to Sagittarius a desire not only to reach the horizon and beyond, but also to encompass and assimilate that which has been experienced. The desire to travel physically and to travel mentally by understanding contributes to and flavors the questing nature of Sagittarius.

The Sagittarian glyph is the centaur, represented by an arrow pointing diagonally upward from a cross. Both symbolize, one metaphorically and the other abstractly, the duality inherent in the quest—in which you are here going there—and particularly the journey from the material to the spiritual (or mental) worlds. Like the centaur, the Sagittarian nature is seen to reside and be subject to the physical, animal world while participating mentally and spiritually in the higher human world. The questing nature of Sagittarius has it always present in the here of the material, but aiming for something higher.

This dual nature is also a function of the mutable modality of Sagittarius. Here, mutability represents the state of living in both worlds or, more commonly, alternating from one world to another. The Sagittarian dilemma is that, while subject to the fiery animal passions, it yearns for the elevated state of understanding or spirituality; yet, when dealing in the abstract realm of understanding or questing after the higher goal, it nostalgically is tugged back to the physical.

At the ego level, the Sagittarian gives in to his/her animal nature and lives to pursue his/her lusts and appetites, which are Jupiterianly large. He/she succumbs to his/her own judgmentalism, rather than trying to truly understand. He/she blindly pursues, driven by his/her own yearnings and desires. In his/her rush to satisfy his/her own ego needs, horselike, he/she tramples others under foot. Yet, with Jupiterian good nature predominating, his/her sin is more often against him/herself—failing to realize his/her full potential—rather than against others.

At the transcendent level, while grounded in the material reality, the Sagittarian heart resides in the spiritual sky. The centaur is transformed into a rider on a winged horse. The steed of the human body now serves the psyche's spiritual purpose. Each horizon is traversed, opening the way to new horizons. Spiritual yearning becomes the psyche's constant state and the spiritual quest its constant activity. All of the psyche's energy is bent like an arrow pointed upward to forthrightly reach its mark.

Capricorn

The essential quality of Capricorn is goal-orientation. The goal-orientedness of Capricorn frequently is manifested as ambition. This is not necessarily driving ambition, although the Capricorn energy is capable of producing driving ambition. Ambition, however, can be seen as the natural outcome of Capricorn's goal-orientation. Other qualities associated with Capricorn, such as a careful and conservative approach, step-by-step procedures and practicality, are characteristics that contribute to the successful achievement of Capricorn ambitions.

Capricorn is ruled by Saturn and also has a strong association with the Mid-heaven. Thus, the Capricorn character tends to be dominated by the super-ego and its concerns, especially the drive for success. Rules and structure, which are the provenance of Saturn, are generally important to the Capricorn-dominated psyche. The Capricorn psyche tends to be structured and organized, sometimes rigidly. Lack of emotionality, a practical and concrete attitude and a preoccupation with tasks are also Capricorn qualities that derive from Saturn's rulership.

Capricorn is the cardinal earth sign. The earth element reinforces the Saturnian qualities within the Capricorn psyche, as Saturn has much affinity with the earth element. The earth element brings groundedness to Capricorn, a strong sense of the practical and an appreciation for the tangible.

The cardinal modality, when combined with the earth element reinforces a drive in the Capricorn psyche to construct and build things. Things of the earth—stone, brick and mud—have always been associated with human building. The active energy of the cardinal modality places the earth element into motion and forms it into shape, resulting in structures being constructed.. The desire to build things that are permanent is also manifested as the Capricornian desire to leave a legacy—something that is useful to society that will remain after the death of the individual. This legacy does not have to be physical, but it must be a tangible form of success in order to be satisfying to the Capricorn psyche.

Capricorn is associated with the tenth house, which is the house of achievement and success. Goal-directedness is a prerequisite for achievement, for no one successfully achieves anything without first formulating it as a goal. All of the earth and Saturn associated elements of Capricorn are needed in order to accomplish goals. The tenth house activities of pursuing success, accomplishing something for society and posterity and, in the process, furthering your own advancement, all become Capricorn traits.

Capricorn's glyph is the mountain goat. The mountain goat symbolizes the climb toward success and rugged persistence in pursuing a goal. It is the characteristic of the mountain goat to proceed up the steep mountain slopes cautiously and step by step. The mountain goat also symbolizes Capricorn's affinity for earth and, particularly, rock. In order to accomplish its goal, the goat, like Capricorn, is willing to endure loneliness and hardship and has the ability to survive in a hostile, yet invigorating, environment. The steady climb to the summit of the mountain goat symbolizes the success that the Capricorn psyche strives for. Yet, success is not equivalent to arrogance for, as the goat willingly bends its knee to gain leverage to climb the slope, the Capricorn psyche is capable of sublimating the ego and its needs in order to achieve its higher goals.

It is not difficult for the ego, however, to take over the Capricorn drive for success. If this happens, then the goat will use its formidable horns to defeat all those who would stand in its way. The goal of accomplishment and success consumes the ego-dominated psyche, causing undue pride if success is achieved and bitterness, envy and self-pity if success eludes the Capricorn psyche. Neither is the ego satisfied with the success that it achieves, but it always demands more. Thus, even when objectively successful, the ego-dominated Capricorn psyche can become self-obsessed and despairing.

At the transcendent level, the Capricornian energy becomes focused on spiritual goals, rather than material pursuits. Even the ostensibly good desire to benefit society and leave some good legacy behind are seen by the transformed Capricorn psyche as being ego-based. Once Capricorn's energy is directed to the transcendent level of action, the psyche will pursue its goals with balanced determination, dedication and humility.

Aquarius

The essential quality of Aquarius is individuatedness. It is the Aquarian's recognition of his/her uniqueness that prompts him/her to want to share his/her knowledge and insight with the world. The sense of social responsibility that Aquarians often feel is born of a sense that they possess an enlightened viewpoint that places them in a uniquely qualified position to lead others. Unlike the Leo, their need is not so much that others recognize and appreciate their personalities as that the ideas that they have received in custody are adopted by others for the betterment of humanity. This insistence in being right, in having direct access to the truth, often comes across as arrogance and, when the Aquarian feels resistance or rejection of his/her ideas, he/she can become petulant or authoritarian.

Aquarius is ruled by Uranus. Uranus' association with the higher mind function contributes to the Aquarian pull toward individuation. Whether the Aquarian is conscious of this pull or not, he/she will often feel set apart in some way. This may be expressed as "marching to a different drummer" or the ego may feel isolated, resulting in a personality dominated by defensive reactions. The Aquarian may revel in his/her unconventionality or he/she may repress this tendency within him/herself for fear of being ostracized and become reactionary and hyper-conventional.

Aquarius is the fixed air sign. This combination is often associated with the tendency to stubbornly hold to ideas and beliefs. It also suggests an importance that is placed on mental and social constructs. The Aquarian tendency is to fix the mental world in place and to want to make social systems concrete. In part, this is a result of receiving revelation fully formed (from the higher mind) and wanting to carry this down and imprint it on the world. From one point of view, the carrying of a higher vision is borne as a service to humanity. From another point of view, the ego is reinforced when it can take those ideas that have formed its identity and see these adopted and carried forth by others. The fixed air quality also suggests the Aquarian difficulty with accepting emotion. Emotions simply have no place in the Aquarian mental construct.

Aquarius is associated with the eleventh house, which is the house of group-identity and of social responsibility. Thus, the Aquarian energy tends to be socially aware and socially concerned, except when the ego's defensiveness forces it into isolation. The association with the eleventh house reinforces the Aquarian tendency to feel the burden of acting for others and assuming that they know what is best for others. It also highlights the Aquarian conflict between individuality and independence, on the one hand, and allegiance to (and the need for acceptance by) the group, whether this be the small group of social peers or the large group of all humanity.

Aquarius' glyph is a symbol variously associated with pouring water or with lightning. In Egyptian myth, the Aquarian figure pours water into the Nile, thus enabling and sustaining human civilization. In Greek and Roman mythology, Aquarius is the cup-bearer for the Gods (Ganymede). The image emphasizes the humanitarian and bringer-from-on-high roles associated with Aquarius. It also signifies the Aquarian connection with the higher mind. One can neither cavort in the Olympian realm nor bring the nectar of higher wisdom to humanity without first attaining a state of individuation that grants access to those higher realms of consciousness.

As alluded to already, the ego can take the seemingly selfless Aquarian role and turn it to its own purposes. Pride and arrogance are typical Aquarian faults. Disregard for the feelings of others, aloofness or a flagrant unconventionality are other signs of the ego's feeling superior due to a heightened sense of one's uniqueness. When authority is not recognized by others, the Aquarian tendency can be to become irritable, aggressive or withdrawn. Fear of rejection by the group also is a consequence of the ego. To compensate for its knowledge of the individual's uniqueness, the ego may attach itself to the values and mores of the group to such an extent that the Aquarian energy manifests as stubborn conventionality.

At the transcendent level, the Aquarian energy must rise above its sense of individuality. Individuation is necessary but one can get stuck at the level of fascination with one's uniqueness on not be able to move on from there. Truly serving society and humanity is one way to rise above this level. However, group-identity and focus on the affairs of the world can also hold one back. The Aquarian energy gains its highest expression when we truly realize that all is simply an outpouring and expression of the Spirit through the Higher Mind. Then, the individual becomes a pliant tool for the Will to act in the realm of matter and existence.

Pisces

The essential quality of Pisces is emotional boundarilessness. It is the underlying feeling of having no boundaries whatsoever that manifests in Pisces' characteristic qualities from unconditional love and compassion to neurotic fear and duplicity. The degree to which the Piscean essence manifests positively or negatively is, to a large extent, a function of the individual's ability to overcome and control the ego. It is also a reflection of the level of comfort that the individual is able to obtain with ambiguity, uncertainty and fluidity, as well as the individual's ability to recognize and establish proper boundaries for the self.

Pisces is ruled by Neptune and the Neptunian qualities of indeterminateness, urge toward transcendence and urge toward dissolution (including self-dissolution) pervade the Piscean essence. The extremely wide scope of expression of Neptunian energy along the negative-to-positive continuum is, also, reflected in the Piscean capacity to manifest its essence from the depths of depravity and addictive behavior to the heights of self-sacrifice and transcendent experience, even being capable of swinging between the two extremes in the same individual. Other Neptunian traits carried over to Pisces include emotional sensitivity, ungroundedness and universality. Prior to the discovery of Neptune, Pisces was seen as ruled by Jupiter and, for a time, Neptune and Jupiter shared co-rulership over the sign. Jupiter's expansiveness contributes to the Piscean sense of boundarilessness and capacity for all-inclusiveness.

Pisces is the mutable water sign. The water element gives the sign its emotional character. Its mutability allows it to navigate the full range of Neptune's expression. Pisceans, generally, see no need to have any fixed position and see no problem with changing their viewpoints and commitments to suit the situation in which they find themselves. Moods, also, can swing back and forth. The temptation to engage in moral relativism is strong and the challenge for Pisces is to keep the ego from exploiting the flexibility inherent in the Piscean essence and playing an endless game of hide and seek from the truth. When positively harnessed, Piscean mutability becomes the platform for complete surrender to the Higher Power--for being, to use a Sufi analogy, as pliant as the corpse being turned this way and that as it is wrapped in the burial shroud.

Pisces is associated with the twelfth house. The twelfth house, traditionally, is associated with things hidden and with isolation, pain and suffering. From this perspective, the twelfth house association is compatible with the Piscean ability to hide the truth, from others and from themselves. It also resonates to a sense of martyrdom, long-suffering, emotional pain or depression that Pisceans often feel. From a depth-astrology perspective, the twelfth house is associated with the end of cycles, which may mean death and rebirth or transcendence and liberation from the cycle of death and rebirth. It represents a time of paying off karmas. Depending on the level of consciousness and perspective, this can either manifest as a sense of being persecuted (resulting in melancholy or paranoid behavior) or in feelings of spirituality and a striving for self-transcendence and liberation.

Pisces' glyph represents two fishes traveling in opposite directions. This symbolizes the duality inherent in Pisces (a quality of its mutability and, also, reflecting the Neptunian capacity to manifest at the dark or light ends of the spectrum). The Pisces energy often finds itself conflicted, pulled in two opposite directions and/or swinging from one pole (often an emotional pole) to the other. Piscean conflicts can be moral or they can arise from the conflicting needs of the self and self-sacrifice.

The fish is also an animal that inhabits the water and this glyph emphasizes the degree to which Pisces is a denizen of the water element. The ocean, with its seeming never-endingness, is most symbolic of the Piscean state. The fish is also a symbol of Christianity, which has dominated the Piscean astrological age of the past two millennia. Christian themes of birth and rebirth (or resurrection), persecution and being born into sin are issues which often accompany the Pisces energy. The two fish moving in opposite directions also suggest the Tao (Ying-Yang) symbol, which also suggests duality and the need to hold opposite energies in balance.

The transcendent expression of Pisces derives from its rulership by Neptune and its association with the twelfth house. The drive to end the cycle of birth and rebirth and the pull toward unlimited transcendence and merging with the One lead to the ultimate Piscean goals. It is a difficult road, however, as the ego has laid traps all along the way.

As much as the self revels in the Piscean sense of boundarilessness, the ego sees this feeling of All-in-Oneness as the supreme threat to its existence. The ego will, therefore, take whatever measures to deny, repudiate or co-opt this sense of boundarilessness. It will even go to the extreme of self-destruction, if need be, for, at least, in the act of self-destruction it is able to affirm that it still exists. When it can, however, it will adopt less extreme measures, employing attachment and possessiveness to graft itself onto Piscean feelings of compassion, universal love and self-sacrifice, appropriating these virtues as its own attributes.

The Aspects

Finally, we will discuss the meaning of the astrological aspects. The aspects symbolize the relationships, or energy flows, that exist between various psychological functions (symbolized by the planets). Thus, the aspects map out the patterns of inner (and, to the extent that your psychic content is projected externally, the outer) stresses and harmonies that make up and affect your psychological state and your personality. The symbolic meanings of the aspects relate to the geometry of points along the circumference of a circle. The relationships between these points (the planetary locations) form angles and (by extension) shapes that are perceived to be more or less harmonious. These geometric relationships then translate to the quality of the energy flows between the planets and the functions they symbolize. Generally, if planets are in aspect, the psychological influence of the functions symbolized by those planets tends to be greater than otherwise.

Conjunction

The conjunction occurs at zero (0) degrees or, in other words, when two planets occupy the same point on the astrological horoscope. An orb on either side of eight (8) degrees is generally given for the conjunction, which means there is a sixteen (16) degree arc on which a planet occupies the mid-point and within which a conjunction may occur. The conjunction generally designates a very close interaction between (or among) the psychological functions symbolized by two or more conjunct planets.

The quality of this close interaction varies depending on the planets involved. Generally speaking, the conjunction of inner planets tends to simply imply an especially smooth or quick connection in the operation of the psychological functions involved. This is generally harmonious, unless two differing spheres of the psyche are involved (i.e., mental and emotional), in which case there may be some capacity for discord. If the Sun is involved in any conjunction, this tends to empower the planetary function that the Sun is conjuncting. A conjunction by the Moon tends to raise the subconscious influence of the planetary function within the psyche.

If transitional or outer planets are involved in a conjunction, then the interaction between the planetary functions may be harmonious or stressful, depending upon the natural relationship within the psyche of the planetary functions involved and, of course, your level of consciousness in dealing with the interaction. Conjunctions by an outer planet may be particularly stressful, simply because most people find the energies symbolized by those planets to be difficult. Outer planet conjunctions also tend to raise the profile of the transformational function, since this is harder for you to ignore when it is interacting with another planetary function. Conjunctions to the calculated points also tend to take the flavor of the conjuncting planet and, especially for the Ascendant and Midheaven, tend to magnify the role symbolized by that planet within the psyche.

Sextile

The sextile is formed at sixty (60) degrees of separation between two planets. This arc divides the circle into six sections and forms a hexagram and a Star of David. An orb on either side of six (6) degrees is generally given for the conjunction, which means there is a twelve (12) degree arc on which a planet occupies the mid-point and within which a sextile may occur. The sextile is considered to be a harmonious aspect. The internal angle formed by a sequence of sextiles is oblique (i. e., soft) and sixty degrees is considered to be geometrically harmonious and balanced (c.f., the three angles of an equilateral triangle).

The sextile symbolizes a helping, friendly energy. It is associated with coming to assistance, with opportunity and with utilization. The sextile often suggests a pathway to relieve the stress symbolized by another planet or planetary aspect. It may also suggest an enhancement of another planet's function. It may symbolize fortuitousness, but it is just as likely that you will have to recognize and act on the opportunity(ies) indicated by the sextile if you are to successfully actualize them and use them to your full advantage. The dynamics of the sextile are symbolized by the typical positioning of sextiling planets in elements that complement each other: Earth and Water, Fire and Air.

Difficulty can arise through the energy transfer symbolized by the sextile in a number of ways. First, you can ignore the opportunity(ies) symbolized by the sextile to your own detriment. Alternatively, you can pursue those opportunities egoistically to the detriment of others (and ultimately yourself). If things come too easily to you, you may take them too much for granted and become complacent, vain or ingrate. Or, you may seek opportunity from a low level of consciousness and, thus, harm yourself spiritually through greed and self-indulgence.

Square

The square is formed at ninety (90) degrees of separation between two planets. An orb of eight (8) degrees in either direction is generally given for the square, meaning that a square can occur for sixteen (16) degrees along an arc on which a planet occupies the mid-point. The square, progressed along the horoscope, divides this circle into quarters, forming a geometric square within the circle.

The ninety-degree angle symbolizes confrontation and conflict. It can be associated with images of two vectors colliding or one broadsiding the other. The right angle connotes resistance, as each vector has equal weight and it is difficult for one to dislodge the other. Thus, the square is traditionally considered to be a malefic aspect and, even from the point of view of depth astrology, it is certainly difficult and challenging.

The square represents two or more psychological functions that are in conflict. When the psychological functions are not being dealt with internally and are projected, the square represents external conflict. The dynamics of the square are symbolized by the typical positioning of squaring planets in elements that are not conducive to each other:

Earth and Fire, Fire and Water, Water and Air, Air and Earth. There is generally such a lack of understanding or correspondence between the squaring functions that compromise or conflict resolution is difficult. Typically, one function will run up against barriers imposed by or associated with the other function represented by the squaring planet.

The square is also involved in two other astrological configurations that are traditionally viewed as difficult or unfortunate. One is the T-square, formed when a planet squares two opposing planets. Here, the difficulty of the opposition is aggravated by the squaring planet. The other is the grand cross. This is formed by four squaring planets (two sets of oppositions), one occupying each quarter of the horoscope. This is seen as the most difficult astrological aspect and connotes great challenges or great calamity.

Although traditionally malefic, depth astrology views the square as potentially positive. The energy symbolized by the square provides the necessary tension in life and in the psyche for growth and development to be stimulated. It provides challenges that demand that you rise to the occasion. The barriers, obstacles and dysfunctional patterns associated with the square can lead to goals for self-improvement or for overcoming your impediments. In fact, it is commonly recognized that an astrological chart without squares may signify a weak personality because that person is not faced with any character-building challenges.

Trine

The trine is formed at one hundred and twenty (120) degrees of separation between two planets. An orb of eight (8) degrees in either direction is generally given for the trine, meaning that a trine can occur for sixteen (16) degrees along an arc on which a planet occupies the mid-point. The trine, progressed along the horoscope, divides the circle into three parts, forming a geometric equilateral triangle within the circle.

The trine is considered to be an easy or harmonious aspect. The triangle is associated with harmonious relationship and the mystical union of the Trinity. This is especially true of the equilateral triangle in which all three sides and angles are balanced. Harmony and compatibility are the hallmarks of the energy represented by the trine. This is symbolized by the fact that, generally, a trine occurs between planets occupying signs associated with the same element.

Trines symbolize an easy flow of psychological energy. Functions associated with planets in trine tend to work well together. Their relationship is marked by peace, balance and harmony. Because the energy flows easily, events associated with the trined functions tend to go off smoothly. Personality characteristics associated with the trined planets tend to be positive because they generally are not encumbered by defense mechanisms designed to deal with stress. A sense of harmony and ease tends to create "good vibes," happiness and contentment both within your psyche and in what you project to the outside world.

The energy patterns symbolized by the trine are able to relieve stresses associated with other astrological configurations. Thus, a trine involving a traditionally malefic planet, especially from a planet that is traditionally viewed as beneficial, can—if you properly actualize the positive energy symbolized by the trine—take some of the "edge" off the more difficult planet. Similarly, a trine to a planet involved in a square or opposition suggests a way of relieving the stress associated with the more difficult aspect.

There are subtle dangers associated with the trine, however. If one or both of the functions symbolized by the trined planets are dysfunctional, then the trine may represent an easy energy path through which that dysfunctionality can spread or be amplified within your psyche. The easy energy associated with the trine can also lead you to become too complacent or to take things too much for granted. This may leave you unprepared for life's crises that are bound to occur. It may also encourage self-indulgence or suggest a life that is insipid because it lacks challenge.

Because of the balance and harmony associated with the trine, this aspect also suggests opportunities for the psychological functions that are symbolized by the trined planets to be involved in a raising of your consciousness. Responding to the harmonious vibration associated with the trine allows you to better develop the transcendent and spiritual dimension of those functions symbolized by the trined planets.

The trine is involved in an astrological configuration, the grand trine, traditionally seen as very fortunate. This occurs when three planets are in trine with one another, all occupying different signs. The grand trine creates a harmonious circular flow of energy among the planets involved and among the already compatible signs and houses that those planets occupy. The trine, along with the sextile, can also be involved in a configuration called the easy opposition when a planet aspects both ends of an opposition.

Quincunx

Although sometimes considered a minor aspect, depth astrology sees the quincunx playing a significant role in the development of the psyche and character. Also called the inconjunct, the quincunx is formed at one hundred and fifty (150) degrees of separation between two planets. An orb of two or three (2-3) degrees in either direction is generally given for the quincunx, meaning that a quincunx can occur for four or six (4-6) degrees along an arc on which a planet occupies the mid-point. Some astrologers, however, may give the quincunx an orb of up to five (5) degrees. The quincunx divides the circle into parts of five-twelfths. Progressed five times along the horoscope, the quincunx divides the circle into twelve parts, forming a geometric twelve-pointed star within the circle. In its connection with the number five, it is associated with Pythagorean mysticism.

The relational energy associated with the quincunx stems from role as the inconjunct, signifying a lack of any relationship between the planetary energies involved. This generally means that you are ill-equipped to handle the progression of energy that normally exists between the functions symbolized by the planets. For instance, a quincunx between Venus and Saturn would indicate that you lack the sense of boundary with respect to your tastes, affections and interpersonal relationships that is normal in most people. You may be innately unable to connect the two functions. Your lack of connectivity may also be caused or exacerbated by the events or circumstances of your early childhood. Regardless, you will often appear "clueless" concerning a functional pattern that is second nature to most people and will need to expend developmental time and energy to connect the psychological dots.

There is also a timing element typically associated with the quincunx. This is because the lack of connection between the two functions symbolized by the quincunxed planets can create a tension that leads to a crisis situation in which you will suddenly be called upon to make the missing psychological connection. Doing so resolves the crisis and helps you attain psychological balance and wholeness. Failing to do so not only may lead to a negative outcome, but generally guaranties a repetition of the crisis in some form or another until you learn the lesson of the quincunx.

The quincunx in the natural horoscope points from the Ascendant to the cusps of the sixth and eighth houses. Through this, the quincunx is associated with both refinement toward perfection (the sixth house) and transformation (the eighth house). Thus, the highest form of resolution of the crisis associated with the quincunx is for the functions symbolized by both of the involved planets to be transformed and perfected.

The quincunx forms an astrological configuration called the Yod, or "Finger of God." This is formed when two planets in sextile both quincunx a third planet. It is this third planet, at the fulcrum of the dual quincunx, to which the Yod points. This indicates that the function symbolized by this planet plays a particularly critical role in your psychological development.

Opposition

The opposition is formed at one hundred and eighty (180) degrees of separation between two planets. An orb of eight (8) degrees in either direction is generally given for the opposition, meaning that an opposition can occur for sixteen (16) degrees along an arc on which a planet occupies the mid-point. The opposition divides the circle into two hemispheres and symbolizes the duality of the psyche and the world.

As its name implies, the opposition indicates that the functions symbolized by the planets involved possess opposite natures and work in opposite directions. Thus, there is implied conflict and often this conflict is "head on." The primary difference, however, between the conflict associated with the opposition and that associated with the square is that the latter is more easily resolvable. This is symbolized by the fact that an opposition will generally occur between planets in complementary signs (Earth and Water, Fire and Air).

The resolution of the oppositional conflict proceeds from the realization that duality is an illusion—albeit, it is the primary illusion from which all other illusions stem. In the polarization of oneness into duality, it is a single essence that is divided, so that common qualities inhabit each pole of the opposition. This is symbolized by the Tao, or Yin-Yang symbol, in which the dark half of the circle contains a white point and vice versa.

The key, then, is to find the commonality within the opposition and realize that each side of the opposition balances and complements the other. Thus, opposition and conflict are transformed into cooperation and harmony. The opposition, once resolved, becomes a source of strength and wholeness. Left unresolved, however, it produces confusion, dilemma and conflict. Rather than resolve the conflict, the ego often seeks to protect itself by erecting a defense mechanism against the conflict (which seems unavoidable and always present—"staring you in the face," as it were).

The ego will usually subconsciously choose one of three defense modes. One is to side with one end of the opposition and confront the other. This gives the ego a sense of righteousness and importance. Another is to suppress one side of the opposition. Here, the ego attempts to hide from the truth and live only on the side of the opposition with which it is most comfortable. A third defense mechanism is for the ego to project the qualities of one of the opposed functions onto someone or something else. The ego, thus, lives out its alter-energy through an external being. In this way, it avoids confronting the conflict within while "actualizing" both ends of the opposition. Inevitably, however, if the energy symbolized by the opposition is strong enough, the subconscious mind will create circumstances through which the oppositional conflict is brought to bear on the ego.